THE DISSENTING READER

Eryl W. Davies introduces a wide range of feminist approaches to the Hebrew Bible: from critics who recover neglected perspectives in the biblical text to those who reject the biblical traditions in their entirety. Davies suggests that the most promising strategy is that which deploys a reader-oriented literary approach to the Hebrew Bible: by focusing on the literary representation of women in the biblical text, some of the subtle ways in which the biblical authors sought to reinforce patriarchal values are highlighted. Davies argues that readers of the Hebrew Bible must don the mantle of the 'dissenting reader' and be prepared to question and challenge the values and assumptions inherent in the biblical text.

Written by a non-feminist, this book demonstrates that feminist biblical critics have offered fresh insights and challenges that need to be pursued and developed by mainstream biblical critics. Davies encourages a fruitful and sustained dialogue between feminist and established biblical scholars in the future.

I
Eirian
a'r plant,
Manon, Llinos,
Gethin ac Osian

The Dissenting Reader

Feminist Approaches to the Hebrew Bible

ERYL W. DAVIES
University of Wales, Bangor, UK

ASHGATE

© Eryl W. Davies 2003

Published by
Ashgate Publishing Limited
Gower House
Croft Road
Aldershot
Hants GU11 3HR
England

Ashgate Publishing Company
Suite 420
101 Cherry Street
Burlington, VT 05401-4405
USA

Ashgate website: http://www.ashgate.com

British Library Cataloguing in Publication Data
Davies, Eryl Wynn
  The dissenting reader : feminist approaches to the Hebrew
  bible
  1.Bible – Feminist criticism
  I.Title
  220.4'46

Library of Congress Cataloging-in-Publication Data
Davies, Eryl W.
    The dissenting reader : feminist approaches to the Hebrew Bible / Eryl W. Davies.
        p. cm.
    Includes bibliographical references.
    ISBN 0-7546-0372-5 (alk. paper) – ISBN 0-7546-0890-5 (pbk. : alk. paper)
      1. Women in the Bible. 2. Bible. O.T. – Criticism, interpretation, etc. 3. Bible.
O.T. – Feminist criticism. 4. Bible and feminism. I. Title.

BS1199.W7 D38 2003
221.6'082–dc21

                                                                    2002038460

ISBN 0 7546 0372 5 (HBK)
ISBN 0 7546 0890 5 (PBK)

Printed and bound in Great Britain by MPG Books Ltd, Bodmin, Cornwall

Contents

Preface

Much of this volume was written during a sabbatical leave which I was granted during February–September 2002, and I am indebted to the authorities of the University of Wales, Bangor, for allowing me this period to pursue my research, unencumbered by the duties of teaching and administration. I am also grateful to my colleagues at the Department of Theology and Religious Studies for undertaking my administrative responsibilities during my absence. I wish also to acknowledge a debt of gratitude to the Alexander von Humboldt Foundation for awarding me two generous grants to undertake research at the University of Tübingen during the summer of 1998, and at the University of Heidelberg during the summer of 2002. I am also grateful to my former colleague at the Department of Theology and Religious Studies, the Revd Dr Margaret E. Thrall, who kindly read the entire manuscript, and made numerous helpful suggestions and constructive criticisms.

The book is dedicated to my wife, Eirian, who has been a constant source of encouragement and support, and to my children, Manon, Llinos, Gethin and Osian, who thoughtfully provided me with some welcome diversions from the often arduous tasks of writing and research.

Eryl W. Davies

Introduction

There can be little doubt that the Bible, over the centuries, has exercised considerable influence on the way in which women are perceived in society. From the opening chapters of the book of Genesis, where woman is created to serve as man's 'helper' (Gen. 2:20–24) to the pronouncements of Paul concerning the submission of wives to their husbands and the silencing of women in communal worship (1 Cor. 14:34–5; Col. 3:18), the primary emphasis of the Bible is on woman's subordinate status. The question addressed by feminist biblical critics is therefore quite simple: how should women in communities of faith react to a document that has served as an authoritative source for the justification of patriarchy? How should they respond to its largely negative appraisal of women and to its oppressive patriarchal emphasis?

Feminist biblical critics have reacted to the problem in a variety of ways and they have developed a number of different strategies to deal with the patriarchal bias of the biblical text. Some have sought to recover neglected traditions and retrieve forgotten perspectives in the biblical tradition and have argued that the Bible is by no means as oppressively patriarchal as is frequently supposed. Others, more radical in their approach, have opted to reject the biblical traditions in their entirety, arguing that they are so immersed in a patriarchal culture that no parts of it are worth redeeming. Between these two extremes, a variety of other approaches have been adopted (see Chapter 2), and each in its own way has contributed some valuable insights to our understanding of the biblical text. The view taken in the present volume is that the most promising strategy developed by feminist biblical critics is that which deploys a reader-oriented literary–critical approach to the Hebrew Bible. The primary emphasis of this study, therefore, will not be on the status or role of women within ancient Israelite society, but on their literary representation in the biblical text. Some of the relevant passages will be analysed for their patriarchal assumptions and for their attention (or lack of attention) to women's experiences and concerns. By focusing on features such as plot, dialogue and characterization, an attempt will be made to highlight some of the subtle ways in which the biblical authors sought to reinforce patriarchal values and endorse women's inferior status.

It will be argued, however, that to expose the text's patriarchal ideology is not enough, for its ideology must also be subjected to examination and critique. Readers of the Hebrew Bible must be prepared to question and challenge the values and assumptions inherent in the text. Instead of being lulled into a passive state of acceptance, they must don the mantle of the 'dissenting reader' and apply what feminist biblical critics have termed a 'hermeneutic of suspicion' to its content.

Of course, such an adversarial reading of Scripture inevitably raises questions concerning the nature of biblical authority. The issue is quite straightforward: can one apply a 'hermeneutic of suspicion' to the biblical text without impugning the authority of the Bible as a sacred text? It will be argued that a critique of the Bible's patriarchal ideology can be justified on inner-biblical grounds, for oppositional female perspectives can be discerned within the text of Scripture itself. Thus, although the Bible is, in many ways, a deeply problematic book for the female reader, there is a sense in which the book contains the seeds of its own solution.

The present volume is written by a non-feminist, but by one who is convinced that feminist biblical critics have brought fresh insights and new challenges that need to be pursued and developed by mainstream biblical scholars. Certainly, feminist criticism has succeeded in undermining some of the principles commonly regarded as axiomatic in traditional biblical scholarship. It has questioned the value of a neutral, objective, disinterested exegesis of the biblical text and has encouraged scholars of the Hebrew Bible to engage in issues of contemporary relevance and concern. It has emphasized the need for an 'ideological critique' of the biblical text and has drawn attention to the ethical responsibility of the individual interpreter. It has highlighted the advantages that can accrue to biblical scholarship of a close engagement with secular literary theory, and it has pioneered new interpretative frameworks in which the discipline can be studied. Although some of the issues raised by feminist biblical critics have been taken on board by mainstream biblical scholars, the powerful intellectual challenge which they have mounted has yet to be felt in its full force. Indeed, there is always a faint suspicion that feminist biblical scholars are engaged in the act of preaching to the converted, and that their scholarly contributions are read and appreciated only by those who happen to share their convictions and sympathize with their approach. It is one of the aims of this volume to break the boundaries between feminist biblical studies and established biblical scholarship, and if the present study succeeds in encouraging a fruitful and sustained dialogue between feminist and non-feminist biblical scholars, it will have more than served its purpose.

Chapter 1

The Patriarchal Bible

Few would deny that the Bible is an overwhelmingly patriarchal book. The opening chapters of Genesis (Gen. 2–3) strike the keynote of woman's inferiority, and it is a note that subsequently resonates throughout Scripture. The biblical traditions reflect a predominantly androcentric world-view which relegates women to the margins and assigns to them a subordinate role in the religious and social life of Israel. The patriarchal ethos is reflected in various complexes of tradition, ranging from the legal texts to the narratives, and from the prophetic texts to the sayings encountered in the wisdom literature.

The Legal Tradition

The laws contained in the Pentateuch appear to be addressed to a society in which only the male was regarded as a legally responsible person. The commandments of the Decalogue, for example, are framed in the second person masculine form,[1] and their content suggests that they were directed at the adult male heads of households who possessed children, cattle, land and servants (Ex. 20:1–17).[2] It was only in exceptional cases that women became the subject of legislation (cf. Ex. 21:7–11, 22–5; 22:16–17); for the most part the law did not address them or even acknowledge their existence.[3]

That the Pentateuchal laws reflect an exclusively male perspective is evident from several enactments. The laws concerning vows, for example, presuppose that women were under the authority of their father before marriage (Num. 30:3–5), and under the authority of their husbands after marriage (Num. 30:6–15), for the vow made by a daughter or a married woman needed the consent of the father or husband to be valid, and if such consent was withheld the vow was regarded as null and void. The inferior position of women is also clear from the laws pertaining to inheritance in the Hebrew Bible, for property was regularly transmitted through the male line, and daughters were permitted to inherit the property of their fathers only if there were no male heirs (Num. 27:1–11; 36:1–12).[4] That the male was treated more favourably than the female is also evident from the slave laws, for the Hebrew male slave was automatically released after six years of service (Ex. 21:2), but no such freedom was permitted the female slave (Ex. 21:7).[5]

1

The subordinate position of women was equally apparent in Israel's cultic legislation, for only males were entitled to serve as priests, and although women were not excluded from cultic observances (Deut. 12:12; 31:12), they were generally regarded as inferior participants in the worshipping community.[6] Central to Israel's cultic laws was the concept of ritual purity, and here, too, significant distinctions were drawn between men and women. According to Lev. 15:16–24, all bodily discharges of males and females were unclean; however, whereas the discharge of a man's semen rendered him unclean only 'until the evening' (v.16), a woman's menstrual discharge rendered her unclean for seven days (v.19). Moreover, after the period of uncleanness was over, both men and women were expected to bring offerings to the priest at the sanctuary, but whereas the men could bring their offerings 'before the Lord' (v.14), the woman who brought an offering was restricted to the entrance of the tent of meeting (v.29), the implication being that only men could come into the divine presence. Also only the male was required to 'wash his clothes and bathe his body in fresh water' (v.13) before approaching the sanctuary; such symbolic cleansing was not required of the female, presumably because she would not be appearing directly before God.

The distinction between male and female was also evident in the laws concerning purification after childbirth, for a woman who had given birth to a son was regarded as unclean for only seven days, whereas if she had given birth to a daughter she would have been regarded as unclean for fourteen days; moreover, in the former case, the mother had to wait for a further thirty-three days before she could participate again in the worship of the sanctuary, whereas in the latter case she was debarred from the sanctuary for twice as long (Lev. 12:2–5).

That the male was more highly regarded than the female is further confirmed by the law of Lev. 27:2–8, which places a monetary value on persons who had dedicated themselves to God. The ruling prescribed that men aged between twenty and sixty were required to pay fifty shekels in order to be released from their vow to perform cultic service, whereas women of the same age were required to pay only thirty shekels. Such monetary discrimination applied to other age groups, too, and a consistently lower value is assigned to the female as opposed to her male counterpart. How the Priestly writers arrived at their calculations is not known, but the discrepancy between male and female is usually taken as a tacit statement of the relative values assigned to each in the culture of ancient Israel.[7]

But nowhere is the woman's inferior position more apparent than in the laws governing marriage and sexual relations, for these are clearly formulated from a male perspective and reflect male interests. For example, in the laws concerning the rape of a virgin who was not engaged to be married,[8] the real victim was considered to be her father, and it was he who received the appropriate monetary compensation.[9] His daughter's plight was further aggravated by the fact that she was required to marry her assailant and – to make matters even worse – he was subsequently prevented from divorcing her (Deut. 22:28–9).[10] That a woman's sexual and reproductive functions were regarded as the legal property of her father or husband is also implied in the law contained in Ex. 21:22, which concerns a pregnant woman who was accidentally hurt and who suffered a miscarriage as a result; in this case it was the husband who was to be compensated for the loss of the unborn child.

The inequality between male and female was further emphasized by the fact that a man was entitled to expect his future bride to be a virgin, though there was no indication that his own virginity had to be intact when he married.[11] If the bride, on her wedding night, could not establish her virginity, she was regarded as having shamed her father and was liable to be stoned to death for her sexual misdemeanour (Deut. 22:13–21).

The double standard applied by the biblical law to men and women was particularly evident in the regulations concerning adultery. Adultery was defined by the law as sexual relations involving a married woman. A husband who had extramarital relations with an unmarried woman, a concubine or prostitute was not regarded as an adulterer; his action constituted adultery only if he had sexual intercourse with another man's wife.[12] Such extramarital relations were regarded as so serious that a jealous husband who merely suspected his wife of infidelity could subject her to a humiliating ordeal that was supposed to prove her guilt or innocence (Num. 5:11–31).[13] Significantly, the husband suffered no penalty if he was found to have accused his wife unjustly,[14] and no parallel ritual was prescribed if a wife suspected her husband of being unfaithful. The laws governing divorce were similarly weighted in favour of the husband, for the dissolution of marriage was regarded in Israel as an exclusively male prerogative.[15] Deut. 24:1 placed the initiative entirely in the hands of the husband, and the law permitted him to repudiate his wife and write her a bill of divorce for no reason other than that he had found in her 'some indecency'.[16]

It is clear from the above résumé that the laws in Israel presupposed a social system in which women were disadvantaged and in which they did not generally possess rights commensurate with those of their male counterparts. Before marriage, the woman appears to have been under the authority of her father, and after marriage she was under the authority of her husband. Biblical legislation seems to confirm that 'from childhood to old age, the Hebrew woman belonged to the men of her family' (Trible, 1976, p.964). It seems highly ironic that the very law codes which demanded such high standards of justice and fairness for the poor and defenceless, and which seemed particularly concerned to protect the vulnerable and underprivileged, appear to have done so little to uphold the dignity, status and self-esteem of women in Israel.

Biblical Narratives

In its emphasis on women's inferiority and submissiveness, the narratives of
the Hebrew Bible in many ways complement the biblical laws. In Gen. 2,
God is depicted as creating man first, then all the lower animals, and finally
– almost as an afterthought – he creates woman to relieve man's loneliness
and to serve as his helper (vv.20–23). Thus, from the outset of the Hebrew
Bible, the male is regarded as 'the original human prototype' whereas
women are viewed as 'secondary and auxiliary beings'.[17]

The subsequent story of Israel is narrated from a predominantly male
perspective. Women are often mentioned in the biblical narratives in a
perfunctory manner, and usually appear as minor characters in a plot that
revolves mainly around the male protagonists. It is almost invariably the
men of Israel who are assigned positions of power and influence in society,
while the woman is usually mentioned only in her capacity as wife or
mother, her primary value residing in her ability to produce (preferably
male) offspring. It is true that a few characters, such as Miriam and Huldah
(both of whom are regarded as 'prophets') and Deborah (who is depicted as
a 'judge' and military strategist), did manage to achieve positions of pre-
eminence, but they were very much the exceptions that proved the rule. By
and large, the narratives reflect a society in which women were perceived as
secondary citizens who were excluded from positions of status and
authority.

On the domestic front, the biblical narratives confirm the impression
gleaned from the biblical laws that marriage in Israel was far from being a
partnership of equals. The wife was expected to remain monogamous,
whereas similar fidelity was not required of her husband, who was entitled
to take a second wife or a concubine (as did Abraham, Jacob, David,
Solomon and others). A man's wife was expected to address her husband as
'master' or 'lord' (cf. Gen. 18:12), the implication being that he 'owned' her
in much the same way as he owned his slaves, herds and land (cf. Ex. 20:17;
21:4). Significantly, the word used in the Hebrew narratives for 'marry' is
lāqaḥ (lit. 'to take'), implying that the bride was viewed as a possession to
be 'acquired' by her husband. That women were viewed in terms of their
'property' value appears to be confirmed by their presence in lists of booty
commonly taken in war (cf. Deut. 20:14; 1 Sam. 30:2, 5; 1 Kgs 20:3, 5, 7; 2
Kgs 24:15) and by the fact that wives were counted along with concubines,
silver and gold as an index of a man's wealth (1 Kgs 10:14–11:8; cf. Bird,
1974, p.64).

Many biblical narratives confirm that the father exercised complete
authority over his daughter. For example, Lot offered his two daughters to
the men of Sodom in order to save his male guests from their lust (Gen.
19:8); Reuel, the Midianite priest, gave Moses his daughter, Zipporah, as a
wife (Ex. 2:21), without any suggestion that she was consulted; Caleb
promised to give his daughter in marriage to whoever succeeded in

destroying Kiriath-sepher (Judg. 1:11–15); and Jephthah sacrificed his daughter in order to keep an oath which he had made to God (Judg. 11:29–40). That daughters were regarded as the possession of their fathers is evident from the fact that they could be bartered for economic gain; their marriage was a matter of negotiation and financial arrangement between the groom and the father of the bride (cf. Gen. 29:18–20; 34:12). Even among royal families, marriage was often a matter of political expediency, and the woman does not appear to have had any role in the negotiations (cf. 1 Sam. 18:17–29).

The biblical narratives also appear to confirm the subordinate position of women within the religious realm. The covenant community was defined as the community of the circumcised which constituted 'every male among you' (Gen. 17:10), and it was the male heads of household who normally represented their families in matters of religious ritual, such as the offering of sacrifice. Thus, for example, in Judg. 13:19 it is Manoah who prepares and offers a sacrifice on behalf of his wife, and in 1 Sam. 1:4 it is Elkanah who sacrifices at the shrine of Shiloh, distributing portions of the sacrifice to his wife and children. Moreover, it is quite in keeping with the male bias of the Israelite cult that the priestly office was confined to males.[18] Although women were not excluded from participating in the worship of the community, the narrative tradition suggests that they assumed only a marginal role. They served 'at the entrance of the tent of meeting' (Ex. 38:8; 1 Sam. 2:22) and, while the precise nature of their service is unclear, it is probable that they functioned as temple servants, performing various kinds of domestic tasks.[19]

Of course, care must be taken not to overemphasize the inferior role assigned to women in the biblical narratives, for there are certainly instances where they appear to have acted with considerable courage, independence and initiative (cf. Num. 12:1–2; 2 Sam. 6:12–23). Moreover, there were probably subtle changes in the status accorded to women over the period during which the Hebrew Bible came to be written. Nevertheless, the biblical narratives do tend to confirm and amplify the inferior role attributed to women in the legal tradition.

The Prophets

The prophets of Israel and Judah often single out women as especially responsible for behaviour which they deemed to be unworthy or morally unacceptable. Amos, for example, castigated the upper-class women of Samaria ('the cows of Bashan', as he called them) for enjoying a comfortable, luxurious and self-indulgent lifestyle at the expense of the poor and helpless (Am. 4:1–3). His contemporary, Isaiah, likewise condemned the flamboyant, ostentatious behaviour of the wealthy women of Jerusalem, who walked around displaying their finery for all to see (Is. 3:16–17). Two centuries later, Ezekiel inveighed against women who prophesied 'out of their own imagination' and who ensnared the people with their lies and divination (Ezek. 13:17–23). Significantly, both Ezekiel and Jeremiah regarded women as the main culprits in the religious apostasy of the people: it was they who wailed for Tammuz outside the temple (Ezek. 8:14), and it was they who presented offerings to false gods and who worshipped the queen of heaven (Jer. 44:15–23).

Further, the prophets deploy female imagery in such a way as to affirm the traditional gender stereotyping of women as physically weaker than men and as dependent on them for their protection and support. Jerusalem (the 'daughter of Zion'), for example, is depicted as a helpless female in need of male rescue (Lam. 1:17; 2:1, 10, 18–19). She is depicted as vulnerable and destitute without a husband and ashamed of being without children (Is. 54:1–6).[20] Babylon is similarly personified as a 'virgin daughter' who is foolish, weak and completely at the mercy of an omnipotent and all-powerful deity (Is. 47:1–15; cf. Darr, 1994, pp.169–74).

Moreover, when the prophets use the marriage metaphor to depict the nature of the relationship between God and his people, the husband (God) is always viewed in a positive light whereas the wife (Israel) is almost invariably viewed negatively (Brenner, 1995b, p.26). In Hosea, for example, God is described as the steadfast, supportive, loving husband, while the Israelites are depicted as his sexually promiscuous and wayward wife. While God (the husband) had fed, clothed and protected his wife (cf. Hos. 2:8–9), she had turned to other lovers for support and had abused the marriage relationship that should have been based on mutual loyalty and trust (Hos. 2:5). In a similar vein, Jeremiah describes the nation's religious apostasy in terms of the once faithful bride who had dishonoured her husband (Jer. 2:1–3:5). The marriage metaphor is also used to depict the people's attempt to forge alliances with foreign countries, and images related to female sexuality are deployed to denounce policies that the prophets deemed to be foolish or dangerous. In two lengthy oracles, Ezekiel portrays Jerusalem (Ezek. 16, 23) and Samaria (Ezek. 23) as Yahweh's adulterous consorts, who had acted in a most depraved manner and who had betrayed their husband's love and trust by offering their sexuality to strangers.

By emphasizing how grossly illicit and unreasonable had been the wife's behaviour, and how patient and long-suffering had been her husband, the prophets were able to justify the punishment which was to be inflicted upon her. Just as the husband was legally within his rights in retaliating against his wayward wife, so God was justified in retaliating against his unfaithful people. He had suffered shame and humiliation on account of their promiscuous and wanton activities, and any act of retaliation on his part was regarded as perfectly warranted and legitimate.[21] Disturbingly, the punishment inflicted by the husband often takes the form of physical violence against his wife, and in their lurid descriptions of the wife's chastisement the prophets' use of sexual imagery occasionally borders on the obscene. In Hos. 2, for example, the husband (God) threatens to strip his wife (Samaria) naked and expose her before her lovers (vv.3,10). Jeremiah similarly compares his country's impending destruction to the shame, humiliation and indignity suffered by a woman whose skirt is snatched above her head and whose private parts are exposed to the public (Jer. 13:20–27). Deutero-Isaiah portrays Babylon as a woman who faces the threat of public exposure and shaming, and who will become the object of contempt and disgust (Is. 47:1–3). But of all the prophets it is Ezekiel who gives the most vivid and detailed description of the nature of the wife's (in this case, Jerusalem's) punishment. Here, explicit sexual language is invoked to describe the fate that awaited her: she is battered, ravaged, abused, disfigured, stripped and publicly humiliated (Ezek. 16:35–52; 23:22–49). In such passages there is not the faintest glimmer of sympathy for the wife; on the contrary, it is implied that, owing to her debauchery and dissolute behaviour, she had brought such punishment upon herself.

By their use of such imagery, the prophets contributed to some of the most vividly misogynist material encountered in the Hebrew Bible. It is striking that the prophets, so often regarded as the great champions of justice in ancient Israel, did so little to challenge sexual oppression, and that those who seemed most concerned about the exploitation of the poor by the rich should have been so oblivious to the exploitation of women which their own words would almost certainly have fostered.

The Wisdom Literature

The wisdom literature similarly displays a disparaging view of women, either by regarding them as nothing more than objects of male desire or by linking them specifically with folly or wickedness. Derogatory remarks about women abound in the Book of Proverbs, where they are variously described as garrulous (22:14), querulous (19:13), idolatrous (2:17), noisy, ignorant and foolish (9:13). A beautiful woman without good sense is likened to 'a gold ring in a pig's snout' (11:22). The contentious woman is like 'a continual dripping on a rainy day' (27:15; cf. 19:13), and it would be better to live in an attic (21:9; 25:24) or in a desert (21:19) than to have to share a house with her.[22]

Of particular concern to the sages was the danger posed by the 'strange', 'foreign' or 'loose' woman (Heb. *'iššâ zārâ*), who was intent upon leading unsuspecting young men astray (Maier, 1995; 1998, pp.92–108). She is described as accosting her victim in the square or the market-place and lying in wait at the corner of the street, under the cover of darkness, to entice him into her house with the promise of pleasure and enjoyment (Prov. 7:10–27). At first she appears to ooze seductive charm; her speech is 'smoother than oil' and her lips are like 'honey', but she eventually turns out to be 'bitter as wormwood' (5:1–4). Many pragmatic warnings are found in Proverbs designed to guard men against her alluring ways. Such women, it is suggested, should be given a wide berth, for those who indulge their desire will be reduced to ruin and will lose their dignity and honour (5:9), not to mention their hard-earned wealth (5:10).

Of course, the view of women presented in the Book of Proverbs is not entirely cynical and pessimistic, for it also contains some positive images of the role and influence exercised by the female. For example, the negative image of the 'strange', 'foreign' or 'loose' woman finds its positive counterpart in Lady Wisdom, and the vices of the former are in many ways counterbalanced by the virtues of the latter (cf. Yee, 1995a, pp.110–26). Further, the mother is occasionally depicted as a teacher who plays an important part, alongside the father, in the nurture and education of her child (cf. 1:8; 6:20). Moreover, the acrostic poem in Prov. 31:10–31 is a paean of praise to the dutiful, wise and compassionate wife, who possesses sufficient authority to direct the servants of her household (v.15) and who is even depicted as engaging in commercial transactions (vv.16, 18, 24). But even in such passages as these the woman's contribution is largely confined to the domestic sphere (spinning, weaving, sewing: vv.13, 19, 22), and such power and influence as she commands are exercised within, and for the benefit of, her family. Although she engages in some activities traditionally associated with the male, such as buying and selling land, her energies are directed at establishing the economic viability of her household, and her behaviour is motivated by the will to gain the praise of her husband and children (vv.12, 28). While it is true that she possessed some measure of authority, it is clear that the real influence was wielded by her spouse, for it was he who had the privilege of sitting among the elders of the land and it was he who was entitled to participate in the important deliberations at the 'city gate' (v.23). Thus, even passages in Proverbs which praise women cannot altogether hide the distinctly patriarchal perspective of the book (see below, p.77).

Koheleth is also commonly regarded as exhibiting a decidedly unflattering attitude towards women, and his anti-female sentiments have sometimes been taken as an indication that he was an unashamed misogynist (cf. Fox, 1989, p.238). Discussions of Koheleth's attitude towards women have tended to focus on Eccles. 7:26–9, which contains comments reminiscent of the statements concerning the 'strange', 'foreign' or 'loose' woman in the Book of Proverbs. Although the passage is obscure, its general drift is reasonably clear. Women are regarded as inherently devious, prepared to use their feminine wiles in order to ensnare their man. The heart of the female is likened to a 'net' and her hands are compared to 'fetters'; clearly, she is dangerous, and any entanglement with her will prove 'more bitter than death'. Only the devout will succeed in escaping her clutches; sinners will inevitably be taken in by her charm. Koheleth claims that his search for an honourable and principled woman had proved futile: 'I have found one man in a thousand worthy to be called upright, but I have not found one woman among them all' (v.28).[23]

The Book of Job is also dominated by a male perspective, although in this instance the patriarchal bias manifests itself by consigning woman to the margins, virtually to the point of ignoring her existence. The numerous dialogues contained in the book are all uttered by men (Job, Eliphaz, Bildad, Zophar, Elihu) and it is finally a male God who responds to Job's lament (Job 38–41). The verbosity of the male debaters in the central poetic section of the book (Job 3–37) stands in sharp contrast to the silence of Job's wife, whose words are confined to one verse, relegated to the narrative framework (2:9).[24] She is represented as urging Job to 'curse God',[25] but the advice which she proffers to her husband is summarily dismissed, and it is made clear that he will have no truck with such foolish and dishonourable woman-talk. Indeed, her words appear to be merely a foil to allow Job to occupy the moral high ground by affirming his belief that the suffering which he has endured was an expression of God's sovereign will: 'Shall we receive the good at the hand of God, and not receive the bad?' (2:10). Not surprisingly, after her initial appearance, Job's wife disappears from view and is all but eliminated from the rest of the book. She is not even named, and although she was afflicted by the same disasters as those which befell her husband (1:13–19), her suffering and loss are not mentioned or acknowledged. That she was viewed as little more than Job's personal possession is evident from a remark which he himself makes in his great confession in chapter 31. Here, Job swears that, if he had committed adultery, then he would willingly let his wife become the sexual property of another man (31:9–12). Of course, the point of the passage is that Job was innocent of all such wrongdoing, but the implication is that, had he been guilty, it is his wife who would have been made to suffer the penalty for an offence which *he* had committed against *her*! Such statements indicate the patriarchal perspective which viewed woman's sexuality as the property of her husband.

The above brief overview of the wisdom literature of the Hebrew Bible suggests that Israel's sages were much preoccupied with women and gender issues. Their world-view was clearly androcentric, and although there are some positive representations of women in the wisdom literature, they do little to ameliorate the predominantly negative view of female sexuality found among the sayings of the wise. Women are either regarded as untrustworthy and potentially fatal for man's well-being (Proverbs, Koheleth) or else their very existence is marginalized or ignored (Job).

Feminist Biblical Criticism

In view of the prevailing androcentric emphasis of the Hebrew Bible, it is hardly surprising that feminist biblical critics have generally regarded it as one of the founding texts of patriarchy.[26] They argue that the values of Western culture have been inspired, directly or indirectly, by the Bible in its various canons and translations, and while they readily concede that various factors have contributed to the establishment of patriarchal power and influence in society, they believe that it would be wrong to deny or minimize the role that the Bible has played in shaping peoples' thoughts and perceptions and in reinforcing sexist attitudes and structures (cf. Schüssler Fiorenza, 1984, pp.xi–xii; 1985, p.129).

Perhaps nowhere have the effects of patriarchal power and influence been more in evidence than in the institutions of the church and synagogue. The statements of Paul concerning the silencing of women in the assembly (1 Cor. 14:34–5) continue to be cited in arguments to prevent women from being ordained and to exclude them from positions of leadership and authority in the church. Similarly, within Judaism, women who feel called to be rabbis often find themselves barred from such vocations and prevented from participating fully in the religious life of the Jewish people (cf. Christ and Plaskow, 1979, p.3; Plaskow, 1990, pp.61–2). Such discrimination, of course, is by no means limited to the religious establishment, for, as many feminist biblical critics have observed, it is equally prevalent within the secular surroundings of the academy.[27] Indeed, concern has been expressed for the long-term viability of feminist scholarship in biblical studies on the grounds that female scholars identified with the feminist cause continue to be unfairly discriminated against because of the supposedly 'radical' views which they embrace (cf. Milne, 1997, pp.43–4).

While it is generally recognized that the ways in which women have been made to feel inferior to men is a complex psychological and sociological problem, feminist biblical critics believe that the teaching of the Bible concerning the role of women has been a significant contributory factor. Part of the problem, of course, lies in the authority invested in the Bible as a sacred text. If the Bible had been read like any other book, its teaching concerning women would have carried little authoritative weight. But the fact is that the Bible has not been read like any other book; rather, it has been regarded over the centuries as the repository of divine truth, and its guidance has been sought and accepted by vast numbers of people throughout the world. Consequently, its teaching concerning the role and status of women has been accepted without question as part of the divinely established order.

Feminists who are also Jewish or Christian scholars thus find themselves in the frustrating position of having to accept as binding and authoritative texts that appear to be incompatible with some of their fundamental beliefs and principles.[28] Their predicament has been well expressed by Letty Russell: 'Are they to be faithful to the teachings of the Hebrew scriptures and the Christian scriptures, or are they to be faithful to their own integrity as whole human beings?' (1985a, p.137). Some feminist scholars, faced with such a dilemma, have opted to reject the biblical teaching altogether, regarding it as irredeemably patriarchal and inherently hostile to women (see below, pp.23–5). Most, however, prefer to view the biblical text as a challenge that must be faced, for they believe that the present-day understanding of the biblical role of women may have far-reaching implications for the rights, responsibilities and role of women in society generally. By addressing the biblical text directly they aim to challenge its assumptions concerning women's cultural marginality and religious subordination, and they believe that, in the process, the role of women in the formal structure of institutional religion can be radically changed. In this way, feminist biblical scholarship is brought into direct contact with issues of current concern, and feminists see themselves as part of a collective enterprise that has as its ultimate goal the elimination of sexual stereotypes and the transformation of cultural values.[29] For them, it is not enough merely to raise awareness of the baneful effects the Bible has had on the position of women in society; rather, the biblical material must be analysed, critiqued and, if necessary, resisted, for they believe that only thus can modern religious institutions be changed and social mores redefined.

One of the first feminist scholars to call for a critical examination of the role that the Bible has played in the degradation of women in Western culture was Elizabeth Cady Stanton (1815–1902).[30] She claimed that every form of religion had denigrated women, but it was primarily the Bible that had kept them in subjugation throughout the centuries and been responsible for denying them some of their basic rights and freedoms. Because of its profound religious and cultural authority, the Bible had been one of the most important influences in defining the status and role of women in society, and so deeply ingrained in the Western psyche was its teaching that it had continually proved to be a formidable barrier to the development of female liberation. Whenever women had complained about their lack of citizenship, or demanded equal access with men to theological training and to the ordained ministry, opponents of women's suffrage had used the Bible as ammunition against them: 'When in the early part of the nineteenth century, women began to protest against their civil and political degradation, they were referred to the Bible for an answer. When they protested against their unequal position in the church, they were referred to the Bible for an answer' (1895, p.8). In brief, the Bible had been used as divine authority for discriminating against women and for justifying their subordination to men.

It was this realization that prompted Cady Stanton, towards the end of the nineteenth century, to initiate her ambitious project, entitled *The Woman's Bible*, much to the indignation of the church and, indeed, the community at large.[31] The aim of the project was to unmask what she perceived as the church's misuse of the Bible and to highlight its invidious role in the oppression of women. Cady Stanton pleaded with the female scholars of her day to contribute to the project, reminding them that 'your political and social degradation are but an outgrowth of your status in the Bible' (1895, p.10). Significantly, however, few responded to her plea, and Cady Stanton lamented the fact that female scholars who were versed in the techniques of biblical criticism did not wish to be associated with her project on the grounds that they feared that their academic reputations would be compromised and that their scholarly ambitions would be thwarted (1895, p.9). Nevertheless, *The Woman's Bible* eventually appeared, in two volumes, in 1895 and 1898, and it contained a compilation of all the sections in the Bible which were of particular relevance to women, accompanied by an appropriate, often acerbic, commentary. Not surprisingly, most of the commentaries on the various passages were written by Cady Stanton herself.

Despite Cady Stanton's labours, however, progress in feminist criticism of the Bible was painfully slow. It was not until 1894 – almost fifteen years after its foundation – that the Society of Biblical Literature voted in favour of admitting its first female members. The fact that there was seemingly little opposition did not betoken a change of heart on the part of its male membership; it merely indicated that the number of women who wished to be admitted was so small that they were not considered as posing a serious threat to the male scholarly establishment (Bass, 1982, pp.6–12). The earliest female members did not deliver papers to the Society, nor did they publish articles in the Society's prestigious journal. Only in the second decade of the twentieth century did women begin to make serious contributions to the academic study of the Bible, and even then their contributions were never self-consciously 'feminist'. During the first half of the twentieth century, gender issues were evidently not regarded as acceptable topics for scholarly deliberations, and consequently feminist biblical studies remained at the periphery of academic discourse (Bellis, 2000, pp.24–5). They were generally regarded with an element of disdain, and viewed as little more than a quixotic indulgence in a harmless, but ultimately irrelevant, hobby-horse.

Such a view, however, changed dramatically during the latter half of the twentieth century. The resurgence of the women's movement in the 1960s not only revived women's struggle for political and civil rights but also gave rise to feminist biblical studies as a new and exciting intellectual discipline. Volumes such as Phyllis Trible's *God and the Rhetoric of Sexuality* (1978) and the anthology *Religion and Sexism* (1974), edited by the Roman Catholic theologian Rosemary Radford Ruether, introduced many women to the new possibilities opened up by feminism for reading and understanding the Bible. Interest developed in what it might mean to read the Bible self-consciously as a woman, and how women in communities of faith should respond to the patriarchal emphasis of Scripture. By the late 1970s, feminist studies had become a recognized area of biblical inquiry and were included in the curricula of many universities and theological seminaries. Since then, the output of feminist biblical scholars has been prolific and sympathy for the type of approach which they advocate has steadily grown within the scholarly guild.

It is true that some feminist biblical scholars, notably Elisabeth Schüssler Fiorenza, complain that the 'woman question' continues to be neglected in what she calls 'malestream' biblical scholarship (1999, pp.3, 33), but the fact is that feminist study of the Bible has by now become a significant area of modern research.[32] One indication of the popularity of the discipline is the wealth of 'feminist companions' to the Bible which continue to appear from the press, and the influence of feminist biblical criticism is clear from the fact that standard works of reference on the Bible and biblical interpretation now include articles on 'feminist theology' as a matter of course.[33] Significantly, when Carol Newsom and Sharon Ringe published in 1992 *The Women's Bible Commentary* (the title of which was a tribute to Cady Stanton's work a century earlier), there were enough female scholars to provide analysis of the relevant passages of every book in the Bible.

Although modern feminist critics (who are predominantly, though not exclusively, female) have approached the Bible from different perspectives and with different presuppositions, there is general agreement among them that the first step in feminist criticism must be an honest recognition 'of how deeply implicated in an oppressive ideology is the Scripture of our own religious communities' (Fewell and Gunn, 1993, p.20). Feminist scholars recognize that there are serious issues in the Hebrew Bible which must be addressed and profound questions which must be answered. How should women react to the repressive and androcentric aspects of the biblical text? How should they broach a document that appears to legitimate patriarchal structures of domination and reinforce cultural stereotypes? How should they respond to texts that are regularly trotted out to emphasize the female 'virtues' of silence and submissiveness? How should they conceive of a deity who is represented almost exclusively in male imagery? The aim of the next chapter will be to examine some of the ways in which feminist scholars, past and present, have sought to respond to these difficult and seemingly intractable problems.

Notes

1   Frymer-Kensky (1992, pp.53–4) argues that the second person masculine form 'you' in the Decalogue is inclusive of both men and women, but the injunction in Ex. 20:17 ('you shall not desire your neighbour's wife') strongly suggests that the personal pronoun refers to men only. Similarly, in the so-called 'casuistic' laws, which typically begin, 'If a man ...' (cf. Ex. 21:7, 20, 26) the term for 'man' in the Hebrew is not the generic term *'āḏām* but the exclusive masculine term *'îš*.

2   The fact that the wife is mentioned between the 'house' and the 'slave' in Ex. 20:17 is regarded by some feminist biblical critics as particularly galling, notwithstanding the fact that in the Deuteronomic version of the Decalogue (Deut. 5:21) she is mentioned first (cf. Brenner, 1994b, p.257).

3   For the view of some post-biblical feminist scholars that patriarchal religion has erased women from history and made them 'non-beings', see Schüssler Fiorenza (1983, p.xviii). Her own tongue-in-cheek definition of feminism is 'the radical notion that wo/men are people' (1999, p.84, n.5).

4   See Davies (1981b, pp.138–44, 257–68). The legislation preventing women from inheriting property may have had far-reaching consequences, since it is probable that only those in possession of their own land could be regarded as full citizens with the

right to participate in the local assemblies (Davies, 1989, pp.361–2). On the rights of daughters to inherit property, see below, pp.89–91.

5   The law governing the release of slaves was subsequently emended in Deut. 15:12 to include both male and female slaves.

6   On the role of women in the cult, see Bird (1987, pp.397–419).

7   Cf. Clines (1990b, p.45). Meyers (1983, pp.585–6; 1988, p.171) argues that the sums accurately reflect the relative economic value of males and females at different stages of life. Thus men aged between twenty and sixty would have been at the most productive stage of their lives, whereas women of this age would have been preoccupied with child-bearing and child-rearing and would have had less time to devote to activities that might bring financial gain to the household.

8   Deut. 22:23–7 concerns the case of a violated betrothed woman, while Deut. 22:28–9 deals with the case of the violated unbetrothed woman. For the view that these laws are not concerned with 'rape' according to the modern definition of the term, see Pressler (1994, pp.102–3).

9   The requirement to pay fifty shekels (Deut. 22:29) merely underlines the economic value of the daughter; once she had been sexually violated, she was clearly not regarded as such a good economic asset as she had been prior to the attack. See Pressler (1994, p.104).

10 The law of Ex. 22:16–17 permits the father to determine whether his raped daughter should be given in marriage to her assailant, but Deuteronomy leaves no option and prescribes that the rapist must marry his victim. A similar directive is found in the Middle Assyrian Laws (Tablet A, pg.55), where the rapist is expected not only to recompense the father of the victim but also to marry her. See Pritchard (1955, p.185).

11 Millett (1969, p.48) observes that in primitive societies the virginity of a woman was important for her intended husband, since it was 'a sign of property received intact'.

12 For a discussion of the sanctions which applied in ancient Israel in cases of adultery, see McKeating (1979, pp.57–72). Adultery by a married woman was regarded as a particularly heinous offence in Israel since it violated a man's absolute right to the sexuality of his wife and placed his paternity in question. This was potentially destabilizing in a society governed by patrilineal kinship structures. See Yee (1992, p.198), Frymer-Kensky (1989, p.92).

13 On the so-called 'trial by ordeal', see Davies (1995, pp.48–57), Brichto (1975, pp.55–70), Frymer-Kensky (1984, pp.11–26), Bach (1993b, pp.26–54).

14 This seems to be the meaning of the phrase 'the man shall be free from iniquity' in v.31. Some have suggested that these words refer not to the woman's husband but to her adulterous consort (cf. Brichto, 1975, p.63), but this seems unlikely, for Hebrew law prescribed the death penalty for both the man and woman found guilty of adultery (cf. Lev. 20:10; Deut. 22:22).

15 The rabbis, who were very aware of the injustice of this non-reciprocal arrangement, sought to mitigate its effects by legislating that the husband must not divorce his wife rashly (cf. Plaskow, 1990, p.62).

16 The precise meaning of the ambiguous term 'indecency' in Deut. 24:1 was much discussed by the rabbis. Shammai took it to refer to adultery, whereas Hillel interpreted it to mean anything displeasing to the husband. The view of Hillel prevailed, and the husband was entitled to divorce his wife 'even if she spoiled a dish for him' (cf. Stagg and Stagg, 1978, p.51; de Vaux, 1965, p.34).

17 See Ruether (1975, p.15). A different reading of the role of the male and female in the Genesis story is provided by Trible (1978, pp.72–143); see below, pp.101–3.

18 It is usually thought that one of the reasons for the exclusion of women from the priesthood was that their menstrual periods were considered to have rendered them unclean (cf. Lev. 15:19–33) and would have caused the sanctuary to be defiled. See Vos (1968, p.193).

19 Bird (1987, p.406) surmises that their work consisted of the preparation of cultic meals,

the cleaning of the cultic vessels, and the sewing of vestments and other textiles for cultic use.

20 For the use of such imagery in the book of Isaiah, see Sawyer (1996, pp.213–14). Weems (1995, p.45) regards such imagery in a positive light (cf., also, Stone, 1992, p.90), but in so far as it portrays women as victimized and dependent it is arguable that it merely serves to perpetuate a patriarchal ethos.

21 Cf. Weems (1995, pp.62–3). Dijk-Hemmes argues that Ezekiel's depictions of the perverse and lewd behaviour of the two metaphorical sisters in Ezek. 23 were designed to impress upon his audience that they did indeed 'deserve the utterly degrading and devastating treatment to which they are exposed' (1993a, p.168).

22 As Fontaine (1992, pp.150–51) observes, the fact that there are no counterbalancing statements concerning the misfortune endured by women who had to live with violent or abusive husbands indicates how one-sided and biased are the views of the authors of Proverbs, who tended to make women the scapegoats for all incidents of domestic discord.

23 Some have attempted to play down Koheleth's contempt and disdain for women by exploiting the grammatical ambiguities of the passage (for a discussion of such attempts, see Christianson, 1998, pp.109–36). However, as Fontaine has remarked, 'interpreters should not and cannot ignore the very real, negative effects on the lives of actual women that the "plain sense" of this text, read over the centuries, created' (1998, p.168).

24 See Klein (1995, pp.186–200). The six words attributed to Job's wife in the Hebrew text are expanded in the LXX into a speech in which she speaks passionately about Job's suffering and her own. There is no reason, however, to suppose that this represents the original text.

25 By uttering such a statement, Job's wife emerges as a kind of mouthpiece for Satan (cf. Job 1:11). Augustine famously claimed that she here plays the role of *diaboli adjutrix*, Satan's unwitting ally. See Penchansky (2000, pp.223–8). For a discussion of Job's wife from a feminist perspective, see van Wolde (1995, pp.201–21).

26 The term 'patriarchy' is defined by Gerda Lerner as 'the manifestation and institutionalization of male dominance over women and children in the family and the extension of male dominance over women in society in general' (1986, p.239). It does not imply that women are totally devoid of rights, influence and resources, but holds that it is men who usually wield power in all the important institutions of society.

27 Schüssler Fiorenza, for example, argues that female scholars identified with the feminist cause are still professionally discredited: 'As one of my colleagues remarked about a professor who had written a moderate article on women in the Old Testament: "It is a shame, she may have ruined her scholarly career"' (1983, p.xvi).

28 As Plaskow (1990, p.ix) has observed, Jewish feminist scholars dwell 'in a state of self-contradiction'. On the 'terrible dilemma' faced by Christian feminist scholars, see Trible (1973, p.31), Sakenfeld (1985, pp.55–64).

29 Schüssler Fiorenza argues that feminism is nothing less than 'a women's liberation movement for social and ecclesiastical change' (1984, p.5).

30 For a discussion of Cady Stanton's contribution to feminist biblical studies, see Wacker (1998, pp.3–7), Schüssler Fiorenza (1993b, pp.1–24).

31 In 1896, even the National American Suffrage Association – which Cady Stanton had co-founded – officially repudiated any connection with *The Woman's Bible* on the ground that it did not wish to offend its membership.

32 For surveys of recent developments in feminist biblical criticism, see Sakenfeld (1985, pp.55–64), Anderson (1991, pp.21–44), Bach (1993a, pp.191–215), Exum (2000, pp.86–115).

33 See, for example, Middleton (1990, pp.231–4), Sakenfeld (1993, pp.228–31).

Chapter 2

Feminist Models of Reading

Feminist critics of the Bible have always been conscious of the dilemma of reading a sacred text whose ideological position with regard to women seems so discordant with their own beliefs and values. They have therefore developed a number of critical strategies to deal with the attitude towards women exhibited in the biblical text. The aim of the present chapter is to review some of these strategies, and, while the survey does not claim to be exhaustive, it does represent some of the most significant approaches that have been deployed by feminist scholars, past and present, who have been concerned with the issue of gender in the Hebrew Bible.

The Evolutionary Approach

One method of dealing with the biblical statements concerning the role and status of women was the so-called 'evolutionary approach'. According to this theory, the customs, beliefs and values enshrined in the Bible emerged gradually over a period of several centuries, and the biblical text bore witness to a progressive refining and modification of Israel's general outlook and perception. The more primitive concepts of the early period inevitably gave way, in time, to more advanced and sophisticated ways of thinking, as Israel felt its way on matters of social, religious and ethical import. This approach was in vogue during the latter part of the nineteenth century and the beginning of the twentieth, and it developed largely as a result of the scientific principle of evolution and human progress. To the mind of the day, familiar with the Darwinian theory of evolutionary development, the idea that the beliefs and values adumbrated in any given period would be subject to the correction of time was regarded as so self-evident that it was seldom seriously questioned in scholarly circles.

Some early feminists welcomed this 'evolutionary' model as a way of exonerating the Bible of any accusation of sexist bias.[1] It was emphasized that the biblical texts covered a period of over a thousand years of Israel's history, during which time significant changes and developments occurred in the rights and privileges accorded to women. Passages which implied their subservient and inferior position belonged, by and large, to the early period of Israel's history, whereas later texts recognized women's legal and social status and evinced a much stronger sense of their inherent dignity and worth.

17

Such a development in Israel's outlook could be seen particularly clearly by comparing the provisions encountered in Deuteronomy (belonging perhaps to the seventh century BCE) with those found in the earlier Book of the Covenant (usually dated in the tenth century BCE). The earlier law code stipulated that only the male slave was to be released after six years' service (Ex. 21:2–11), whereas the later law stipulated that male and female slaves were to be treated equally and that both were to be liberally provided for upon their release (Deut. 15:12–18). Again, in the earlier law (Ex. 20:17), the wife was regarded as no more than a chattel, but in the later Deuteronomic version she was deliberately distinguished from the chattels and was regarded as a person in her own right (Deut. 5:21). Further, the single command not to take advantage of the widow in the earlier code (Ex. 22:22–4) was considerably amplified in Deuteronomy by the inclusion of provisions permitting her to glean the fields and vineyards of others (Deut. 24:19–21) and injunctions preventing anyone from taking her garments in pledge (Deut. 24:17).

The evolution in Israel's thinking could also be seen in the biblical narratives. For example, polygamy was a phenomenon which was encountered primarily in Israel's early narrative traditions,[2] but as the nation advanced in its outlook the custom gradually fell into desuetude and was eventually replaced (precisely when is not known) by the practice of monogamy. The two creation accounts contained in the beginning of Genesis were similarly thought to evince a significant development in the status accorded to women. In the earlier text (Gen. 2:4b–25), usually dated to approximately the ninth century BCE, the creation of woman was regarded almost as something of an afterthought, and her subordinate position was emphasized by the fact that she was created from the rib of man as a helpmate to cure his loneliness; but in the later account (Gen. 1:1–2:4a), belonging perhaps to the fifth century BCE, man and woman were created simultaneously in God's image and likeness, and were regarded as equal partners participating in a common enterprise.

One of the primary advocates of the 'evolutionary' approach among more recent scholars was Thierry Maertens, whose volume, significantly entitled *The Advancing Dignity of Woman in the Bible*, appeared in 1969.[3] Maertens endeavoured to trace a progress in the status of women from the early documents of the Hebrew Bible, through the literature of the inter-Testamental period, and into the New Testament. He concluded that ten centuries of evolution in Israel's thinking could clearly be seen in the biblical documents, for the attitudes towards women encountered in the later texts were decidedly more enlightened and sophisticated than those found in earlier traditions. In the early texts, for example, marriage was either a matter of convenience or the subject of commercial transactions (cf. Gen. 29:15–20; 1 Sam. 18:17–29), but in later texts (cf. the Song of Songs 8:6–7), the bride was loved for herself, and marriage was a matter of personal choice rather than barter (Maertens, 1969, p.113). By the third century BCE, Israel's outlook had advanced to such an extent that a woman could have a whole book devoted to her (Judith), and could be depicted as possessing servants, livestock and land (Judith 8:7); moreover, she was able to speak freely to the elders of the city and take an active interest in public affairs (Judith 8:9–36; cf. Maertens, 1969, pp.100–102).

The development in women's status was regarded by Maertens as having reached its climax in the ministry and teaching of Jesus, who overturned some of the fundamental tenets of his Jewish heritage and rejected its double standards which discriminated unfairly against women.[4] Jesus declared that the sole prerogative of the husband to sever the marriage bond was unjust, and he recognized that a wife had the same right to divorce her husband as he had to divorce her (Mk 10:2–12). Moreover, his reaction to the woman with the haemorrhage who touched his garment showed his complete disregard of the taboo which declared blood to be unclean (Mk 5:25–34). Jesus' teaching paved the way for greater participation of women in the leadership of the Early Church, and various indications in the Book of Acts (18:26) and in Paul's letters (Rom. 16:1–16; Phil. 4:2–3) suggest that they were prominent among the early Christian leaders. Although Paul himself occasionally gave the impression of being less favourably disposed to women, his ultimate vision was of a common humanity in which ethnic, social and sexual differences would be transcended (Gal. 3:28).

According to adherents of the 'evolutionary' approach, therefore, to blame the Bible for the inferior status accorded to women was both unfair and misguided; indeed, far from condemning the biblical teaching for its perceived misogynist stance, it should be applauded for elevating the status of women and for pointing the way towards the ideal of true equality. Of course, it was true that the Bible did contain *some* passages that appeared to denigrate the position of women, but such passages were problematic only if the progressive nature of its revelation was ignored. Once the biblical texts were placed in something approximating their true chronological sequence, and the attitude towards women was viewed in the context of the development of biblical revelation as a whole, the Bible would be seen to reflect a growing recognition of the rights and dignity accorded to the female.

Although Maertens' volume represents a spirited defence of the biblical teaching concerning women, few feminists today have been persuaded by the 'evolutionary' argument, and most recognize that this strategy is beset with serious flaws. In the first place, it is by no means clear that the biblical documents do, in fact, bear witness to a gradual development in the status accorded to women. Carolyn Pressler (1993), for example, has examined the status and role of women as reflected in the family laws of Deut. 12–26, and has rejected the view that these laws display a more humane attitude to women than that exhibited in earlier collections, or that they mark a significant improvement in women's domestic or legal status. Further, Phyllis Bird has demonstrated that the fullest and richest evidence for women's cultic activity is found in the literature of the pre-monarchic period, which also provides the richest portrait of women in leadership roles (Ex. 15:20–21; Num. 12:1–8; Judg. 5:7).[5] The 'evolutionary' theory is further undermined by the fact that some of the later texts betray a far more pronounced hostility towards women than anything found in the earlier sources, as is clear, for example, from Ben Sirach, whose frequent pronouncements in this regard are unashamedly misogynistic (Sir. 25:16, 24–6; 26:7–8; cf. Camp, 1997, p.102).

Even in the New Testament, it is doubtful whether the status of women had progressed to a significant degree, for the pronouncements of Paul concerning the role of women seem decidedly negative in their emphasis,[6] and the so-called 'household codes', which are usually thought to reflect the social mores which prevailed in the Early Church, are noted for the restrictions and constraints which they imposed upon women.[7] In many respects it seems that the position of women was no more exalted in early Christianity than in Judaism, and there may be an element of truth in the comment by Cady Stanton that their inferior status was 'more clearly and emphatically set forth by the Apostles than by the Prophets and the Patriarchs'.[8] This is not to suggest that there was a gradual regression in the views regarding women found in the Bible, merely that it is misleading to speak in terms of an historical, evolutionary development. Probably different opinions concerning the role and status of women were held by different groups in Israel simultaneously, and it might be more appropriate to think in terms of 'a fluctuation of liberation and suppression, power and powerlessness, side by side' (Schroer, 1998, p.104) rather than in terms of a steady, gradual development which can be traced with any degree of confidence within the biblical documents. For these reasons, feminist biblical scholars, while recognizing that women's social and legal status changed in subtle and complex ways over time, have tended to look for other solutions to the problem posed by the denigration of women in the Hebrew Bible.

Cultural Relativism

One such solution favoured by some feminist biblical scholars is that associated with the cultural relativists.[9] This approach emphasizes that the Hebrew Bible evolved out of a particular historical, social and cultural situation and must be read in the context of the society for which it was written. The biblical writers were children of their time, and it was inevitable that they should reflect the attitudes, outlooks and beliefs appropriate to the people of their age. Modern readers of the Bible must therefore accept the historical time-conditionality of its writings and recognize that they are often expressive of ways of thinking which are no longer our own. Thus, before any judgment is passed on the biblical authors for the particular views which they embraced, they must, in all fairness, be considered in the context of the period and culture to which they belonged.

Such a strategy has been welcomed by some feminist biblical critics as providing a solution to the problem caused by the presence in Scripture of statements that are degrading or condescending in their attitude towards women. The offending passages, it is argued, are merely a reflection of the beliefs and customs of people who had very different frames of reference from our own and who belonged to a cultural system far removed from the one which we inhabit. That cultural system was characterized above all by patriarchy, and the starting-point for any feminist reading of the Bible must be a recognition that it originated in a male-dominated world and that it was designed to promote patriarchal interests and needs.[10] Once viewed in this light, the biblical writers are conveniently exonerated of any 'sexist' attitudes which they may have exhibited, for their views were merely a reflection of a culturally inherited and deeply ingrained bias which was inevitable, given the nature of the society to which they belonged.

Further, it is argued that, once the biblical pronouncements concerning women are seen in their proper sociohistorical context, they may not be quite as discriminatory as they might at first appear. Gender differences that may strike us as oppressive or hierarchical may not have been so perceived in ancient Israelite society (cf. Schroer, 1998, pp.90–91). Carol Meyers cites as an example the role of women in the domestic realm. She argues that, in ancient Israelite society, where many infants died prematurely, large families were needed to offset the high death rate, and women's biological contribution in conceiving and giving birth to children would have been regarded as just as important as the contribution of men in the public sphere.[11] Thus, to regard the confinement of women to the home as a sign of their inferiority would be to impose modern standards and perspectives on a culture that existed in the distant past and would be to misunderstand the nature of ancient Israelite society.[12] Similarly, the exclusion of women from the priesthood may not necessarily have been regarded as a denial of their rights or a sign of their inferior status; rather, it was a recognition that their energies might more profitably be directed to the crucial tasks of child-bearing and child-rearing (Meyers, 1988, pp.36, 163). Such patterns of gender behaviour were established in biblical times to meet the exigencies of daily life, and to regard them as necessarily indicative of a hierarchical gender structure would be to indulge in an anachronistic error. Practices and customs which existed in ancient Israel must not be removed from the total cultural context which gave rise to them, and Meyers insists that only when the reader is made aware of the 'antiquity of the texts' and 'the otherness of the society that produced them' can a fair, meaningful and balanced evaluation be made of the role of women in the biblical writings (1988, p.34).

Now it cannot be denied that such an approach has a certain logical appeal. We intuitively accept that what is regarded as right and proper varies from culture to culture and from age to age, and we recognize that the Bible, as a cultural artefact, merely reflects the prevailing world-view of its time. However uncongenial to the modern mind is its stereotyping of gender roles, we tend to accept it as part and parcel of the general culture from which the biblical writings emerged. We may well feel that the biblical writers have been unfair to women, but we recognize that *we* would be unfair to *them* if we failed to see them in the context of their predominantly patriarchal culture. After all, it is hardly their fault that intervening historical developments have changed people's outlooks and perceptions, and it would be invidious to blame them for espousing views which we ourselves would almost certainly have embraced had we been living in their time and been part of their culture.

But while the strategy associated with the cultural relativists is ostensibly appealing, it is not without its problems. In the first place, it implies that the biblical injunctions have only a limited validity, since they were ultimately binding only upon the society for which they were intended. For the cultural relativists, the biblical injunctions concerning women belong to the Bible's culture-bound pronouncements and were not intended to be wrested from their historical and cultural moorings and transported across the centuries as though they were equally applicable today. Rules derive their legitimacy from the social contexts out of which they evolve, and customs and attitudes which may well have been viewed as perfectly proper and valid in one age may not necessarily be so regarded in another. But such a view of the biblical material inevitably tends to highlight the distance that separates the biblical writers from the modern reader. Reading the Hebrew Bible as an historically-conditioned book courts the risk that it may come to be regarded as nothing more than a museum-piece, an antiquated relic of the past having little or no relevance for issues of present-day concern.

Moreover, the view that we should evaluate biblical norms against the background of the period and culture from which they emerged may sound perfectly logical in principle, but it is an ideal which remains largely elusive. However hard we try to become part of the audience for whom the biblical writings were composed, the fact is that time and distance have intervened and provided us with conscious or unconscious perceptions which we can do nothing to obliterate. Consequently, we are almost bound to evaluate past norms on the basis of those of our own age and culture.

Further, the approach of the cultural relativists – especially as practised by some of its early adherents – tended to encourage a rather patronizing attitude towards the biblical writers, for they were prone to claim (either explicitly or implicitly) a kind of superiority for their own, supposedly more enlightened, position. Such an attitude is well exemplified, for example, by Cady Stanton's perfunctory dismissal of the Pentateuchal laws relating to women as decrees which emanated 'from the most obscene minds of a barbarous age', and by her appeal to 'the common sense of a more humane and progressive' epoch.[13] It is little wonder that more recent feminist critics have criticized such intellectual arrogance as ill-judged and misconceived, and have pleaded for a more tolerant approach which refrains from denigrating those values that happen to conflict with one's own.

It is all too easy, in discussing the biblical passages which appear demeaning to women, to retreat into the safe haven of cultural relativism, stressing how time-bound and culturally dependent the writings of the Hebrew Bible are. The fact that its provisions were addressed to a particular situation does not mean that they should therefore necessarily be excused or exonerated. To concede that Hebrew society was thoroughly misogynist, and then seek to defend it by saying, in effect, 'but so were the surrounding cultures at the time', is not a particularly satisfactory solution to the problem caused by the patriarchal emphasis of Scripture. It is rather like trying to exonerate the divine commands to annihilate the Canaanites by saying, 'Not to worry! This was the normal practice at the time and this is how all enemy nations were treated during this period'! The strategy gives the impression of being merely a convenient way of side-stepping the problem caused by the presence in the Hebrew Bible of passages which happen to conflict with current values and judgments, and it implies that if we try hard enough to see events and customs in the context of their own period and culture we can find an excuse for virtually everything in it.

The Rejectionist Approach

A far more radical strategy of dealing with the patriarchal bias of the Bible is to reject it as an authoritative text. Within the feminist movement, one of the main advocates of the 'rejectionist' approach has been the former Roman Catholic scholar Mary Daly, whose book *Beyond God the Father* first appeared in 1973.[14] Daly argued that the Bible and the entire Judaeo-Christian tradition was irredeemably sexist and had proved over the centuries to be damaging to women's interests and concerns. The patriarchal texts had all but ignored women's experiences and had effectively erased them from history and made them into nonentities. On the other hand, they had fostered the image of God as the great patriarch in heaven and as the all-powerful male ruler, and this image had been used to legitimate women's social and religious subordination and to promote male dominance and superiority. If God the 'father' was in 'his' heaven ruling over 'his' people then it seemed only right and natural that human society should be ruled by men and that women should assume a subordinate role. In this way, religious dogmas were used to justify existing social structures and to sustain their plausibility (Daly, 1973, p.13).

Such blatant discrimination, according to Daly, was woven into the very fabric of Israelite society and was inseparable from the essence of the religious tradition represented in the Bible. There was therefore little point in purging the Judaeo-Christian tradition of some of its patriarchal elements, or eliminating from Scripture particular texts that might offend feminine sensibilities; rather, the Bible as a whole was to be rejected, since it was sexist to the core and was uniformly degrading in its attitude towards women.[15] It had served merely as an instrument to keep women in their place and to thwart any desire on their part to improve their status. The only option for feminists was to reject the authority of the Bible and to look elsewhere for ways of 're-imaging and re-naming ... the "world" bequeathed to us' (1973, p.165).

Such a radical feminist critique led Daly to move beyond 'God the Father' to a post-Christian/Jewish feminism, capable of conquering the evil of patriarchy and transcending its predominantly negative impact. For Daly, this seemed a perfectly natural and logical step since, in her view, few contemporary feminists showed any interest in, or allegiance to, traditional forms of institutional religion. Nevertheless, Daly was convinced that feminists were not totally lacking a spiritual consciousness, and she believed that this consciousness could be harnessed by them to find a different form of religious expression. The form favoured by Daly herself was expressed in terms of a 'cosmic covenant', by which feminists could experience a living harmony with the self, the universe and God (1973, pp.155–78). Participation in the transcendent dimensions of feminism would bring about a 'refusal of our own objectification' (p.177) and would open up human consciousness to a desire for a non-hierarchical and non-oppressive society (p.190). Without the power of such a transforming vision, women would be condemned to remain in their ancient bondage and would never be able to transcend the subservient position into which they had been cast by centuries of patriarchal conditioning.

The rejectionist approach advocated by Mary Daly, however, has not generally won widespread support, and few even among the most ardent biblical feminists have been prepared to abandon the Judaeo-Christian legacy in its entirety. Such an approach fails to acknowledge that the Bible is read and preached as an authoritative text in countless communities of worship throughout the world, and that it continues to exercise considerable influence upon contemporary society. Feminists therefore recognize that they cannot afford to relinquish the Bible and the biblical faith, and most are of the view that they are more likely to win over converts to their cause by advocating a feminist critique of Scripture from within the Judaeo-Christian tradition itself (cf. Russell, 1985a, pp.138–40; Collins, 1985, p.8). Moreover, they recognize that the Bible is not just a religious document of interest only to communities of faith; it is a profoundly political book which has informed – and continues to inform – the ways in which men and women relate to each other in the Western world (cf. Schüssler Fiorenza, 1984, p.xi). The values which it embraces have been internalized subconsciously by people who would claim no particular religious allegiance and who would not regard the Bible as a sacred text. Thus rejecting the Bible would largely be a symbolic and meaningless gesture, for there would still remain an indissoluble link between the politics of male domination that has permeated Western culture and the representation of women found in the biblical text.

Moreover, many feminist critics have questioned whether the biblical tradition is, in fact, as irredeemably patriarchal as adherents of the rejectionist approach suggest. On the contrary, they claim to have found in the Bible much of lasting value for women that is worth salvaging, and recognize that their lives have been enriched, sustained and empowered by its teaching. While the Bible may contain material that is unhelpful and uncongenial to the feminist cause, it also contains much that is supportive of woman's dignity and worth. To reject the biblical tradition *in toto* was thus regarded as tantamount to throwing out the proverbial baby with the bathwater. Daly had failed to appreciate the positive value which the Bible might have in empowering women to oppose male domination. Just as liberation theologians had discovered in the Bible texts that supported their fight for freedom, so feminist scholars might find in it passages that were helpful for women in their struggle for emancipation. The weakness of the rejectionist approach was that it viewed the Bible only as part of the problem, whereas in fact it might also prove to be part of the solution (cf. Schüssler Fiorenza, 1983, pp.xviii–xx; 1998, pp.26–8; Tolbert, 1983a, p.120).

The rejectionist strategy was also viewed by many feminists as too rigid and uncompromising in its approach. Women were invited either to accept Scripture, with its androcentric values and its male representation of the deity, or else to reject the Bible and discard the old, outworn baggage represented by the Judaeo-Christian heritage. But most Jewish and Christian feminists did not tend to regard the Bible as a 'given' which they must either accommodate themselves to completely or reject outright; rather, they recognized that the traditions which they embraced were flexible and fluid and were continually changing to meet contemporary needs (cf. Plaskow, 1990, pp.xi–xii). Hence feminism was not to be regarded as a phenomenon which was necessarily in conflict with the Judaeo-Christian tradition; to be sure, there were often tensions between them but, provided an appropriate methodology could be applied to the biblical text, such tensions could be satisfactorily resolved.

For these reasons, the radical feminist critique offered by Daly has been regarded as too extreme and reactionary for most feminist biblical scholars, and the majority have preferred to adopt other strategies to deal with the patriarchal bias of Scripture. These strategies involve retaining the Bible and searching within the biblical tradition for more positive and constructive alternatives to the Bible's predominantly patriarchal emphasis.

The 'Canon-within-a-canon' Approach

This strategy is one which has often been used by biblical scholars who have been troubled by the morally unacceptable passages of Scripture. They recognize that today's readers are bound to find in the Hebrew Bible material which they will reagrd as offensive or unpalatable, and so they invite them to sift through the biblical texts in search of what they might find useful and valuable as a source of moral guidance in their daily lives. The material which they deem to be edifying can be retained, while that which they regard as objectionable may be discarded. Passages of a morally dubious ethical value, such as those which prescribe the complete annihilation of the Canaanites and other nations at the express command of God (cf. Deut. 7:1–2) may conveniently be shunted to one side, allowing readers to concentrate instead on texts which contain lessons of a more salutary nature, such as the importance of beating swords into ploughshares and spears into pruning hooks (Is. 2:4). In effect, readers of the Bible are invited to form their own 'canon' of texts based on the wider canon of Scripture, and by adopting this approach they are free to focus upon those features of the biblical tradition which they regard as central and relevant to their faith.

Such a strategy, not surprisingly, has proved particularly appealing for feminist critics offended by the deprecatory attitude to women exhibited in much of the biblical material. The approach invites them to sideline the more objectionable statements of Scripture and to highlight instead those which view the female in a more positive light and which offer a welcome alternative to the predominantly patriarchal perspective. This strategy characterized the type of feminist hermeneutic commonly deployed in the nineteenth century when, in their struggle for emancipation, feminists tended to embrace biblical passages supportive of female liberation while carefully side-stepping passages of a more oppressive nature (Gifford, 1985, pp.16–18). Texts such as Gen. 2:21–3, which appear to affirm the subordination of women, were quietly ignored in favour of texts such as Gen. 1:26–7, which presupposed a more egalitarian view of the sexes; passages in the Pauline epistles which demanded the submission of women to their husbands (cf. 1 Cor. 11:2–16; 14:34–5) were cast aside in favour of the apostle's more positive statements regarding the equal status of male and female (Gal. 3:28). By means of such dexterous proof-texting, feminists were able to argue that the Bible was not as sexist as was often supposed, and that it contained material which could be used as a valuable weapon in the battle for female emancipation.

Recent feminist scholars have advocated a more refined version of the 'canon-within-a-canon' approach. While they would certainly not go so far as Cady Stanton and argue in favour of an 'expurgated edition' of Scripture (1895, p.61), they do conceive their task as being to recover and articulate the positive images of women recorded in the Bible, and to seek out, in the words of Francis Watson, 'valuable building-material ... in the midst of all the patriarchal rubble' (1994, p.190). Among modern feminist scholars, one of the leading advocates of such a strategy has been Phyllis Trible, who has likened her own approach to Scripture to the woman in Jesus' parable who persistently searched for a coin which she had lost (Lk. 15:8–10): 'Much as the ancient housekeeper of the New Testament, while possessing nine coins, searched for the tenth which she had lost, so we too, while acknowledging the dominance of male language in scripture, have lit a lamp, swept the house, and sought diligently for that which was lost' (1978, p.200). According to Trible, one of the dimensions of biblical faith which has been 'lost' over the centuries, and which needs to be rediscovered and restated by modern feminist biblical critics, is the use in the Hebrew Bible of female metaphors applied to God. While depictions of God as father (Ps. 103:13), husband (Hos. 2:16), warrior (Ex. 15:3) and king (Ps. 98:6) are familiar enough, Trible argues that we must not lose sight of the fact that the biblical authors also used female metaphors to depict the deity – metaphors such as the pregnant woman (Is. 42:14), mother (Is. 66:13) and midwife (Ps. 22:9).[16] Such female metaphors, according to Trible, may unfold new dimensions of the biblical portrayal of God and may serve to broaden and enrich our understanding of the biblical deity as both male and female. The patriarchal emphasis of Scripture is thus modified by highlighting traditions which have been repressed by biblical authors and neglected by generations of subsequent commentators.

Unlike advocates of the rejectionist approach, therefore, adherents of the 'canon-within-a-canon' strategy argue that the Hebrew Bible contains material that is worth salvaging, and that it provides a message which is both liberating and relevant for women in their struggle for emancipation. Instead of being overwhelmed by the negative aspects of Scripture, feminist biblical critics should highlight its positive aspects; instead of berating the Hebrew Bible for its unrelenting patriarchal emphasis, they should celebrate the fact that a feminine viewpoint has survived in the tradition despite all the efforts to suppress it. The Hebrew Bible contains powerful and admirable images of women, and once these images are given the recognition they deserve, the Bible can be redeemed from what Trible has called its 'bondage to patriarchy' (1995, p.8) and reclaimed on behalf of those who have been excluded from it.

Trible herself sees such positive images in the Book of Ruth, which extols women's initiative and independence in a male-dominated world, and in the Song of Songs, where the voice of the female (in contrast to her male counterpart) is direct, articulate, steadfast and enterprising, and where there is no suggestion of male domination or female subordination (1978, pp.144–99). Others have drawn attention to such formidable figures as Miriam, the prophet (Ex. 15:20) who had the courage to reproach Moses for his exclusive claim to divine revelation (Num. 12:1–2);[17] or Deborah, the military strategist and heroic leader whose presence on the field of battle was regarded as a guarantee of success (Judg. 4:4–16; 5:1–22); or Huldah, the prophet who was consulted by the king's emissaries and whose crucial decision led to Josiah's religious reform (2 Kgs 22:14–20).[18] By focusing on such positive images of women, adherents of this strategy argue that the Hebrew Bible is not entirely devoid of a female perspective, and while they recognize the overwhelming patriarchal stamp of Scripture, they believe that there are fundamental impulses in the biblical tradition that are representative of more inclusive ways of thinking.

But while the strategy of 'maximising the positive' (Joyce, 1990, p.3) has many attractions, the approach is not without its potential drawbacks. In the first place, by inviting the reader to exploit a partial view of Scripture, and to focus on specific texts to the exclusion of others, it inevitably courts the risk of violating the integrity of the biblical message as a whole. It tends to absolutize certain texts and relativize the value of others and, as Schüssler Fiorenza has observed, the danger of advocating such a reductionist method is that it fails to do justice to the richness of the biblical material and may even distort the very essence of its teaching.[19]

Secondly, the strategy sometimes gives the impression of being merely a convenient way of permitting feminist critics to shake off the liabilities of the Hebrew Bible and relieving them of the difficulty and embarrassment caused by the presence in Scripture of texts which they wish were not there. As such, the approach at times seems overly simplistic: specific passages are categorized as either 'oppressive' or 'liberating', as either 'for' or 'against' women, and the impression given is that all we need do is add up the sexist and non-sexist passages in the Bible and declare that the non-sexist has won (cf. Plaskow, 1990, p.xiii). In fact, as will be demonstrated in the course of the present study, the biblical passages relating to gender issues are far more subtle and nuanced than is often supposed.

Thirdly, adherents of the 'canon-within-a-canon' strategy are not always sensitive to the fact that positive appraisals of women in the Hebrew Bible may actually serve to confirm and reinforce the patriarchal ideology of the biblical authors. For example, Ruth's allegiance to Naomi may appear to suggest that she was acting merely out of female solidarity, but the narrative implies that her actions were ultimately intended to serve the interests of patriarchal continuity.[20] Even in the Song of Songs, which seems to take an egalitarian stance on the issue of gender relations, there is a suggestion that sexual freedom was essentially a male prerogative, and that the woman who acted on her own impulse ran the risk of being abused and shamed.[21] By drawing attention to such passages, adherents of the 'canon-within-a-canon' approach may inadvertently be re-inscribing the patriarchal ideology implicit in the text, and consequently the strategy deployed by them may prove to be entirely counterproductive.[22]

But the main problem for feminist critics who adopt this approach is the very paucity of usable tradition within the biblical material. The fact is that there are only a limited number of female figures in the Hebrew Bible that can be elevated to heroic status, just as there are only a limited number of female metaphors for God which can be used to highlight his 'maternal' character (Bach, 1993a, pp.198–9; 1999, p.xv). To inflate the significance of such elements out of all proportion merely smacks of special pleading. However many figures such as Deborah and Miriam are trotted out of the

Hebrew Bible, they cannot blind us to the overwhelmingly patriarchal character of the biblical text (cf. Ackerman, 2002, pp.47–51), and however many female metaphors for God are discovered they can do little to alter the predominant picture of Yahweh as a male deity (cf. Brenner, 1997a, pp.68–9). For these reasons, the 'prettified canon' favoured by adherents of this strategy cannot ultimately resist the patriarchal agenda of the biblical authors (cf. Bach, 1993a, p.197), and some have wondered whether the procedure of salvaging non-patriarchal fragments from the biblical text and gleaning small consolations from isolated passages is worth all the effort.[23]

The Holistic Approach

In many respects, this strategy is diametrically opposed to the 'canon-within-a-canon' approach. According to this view, to single out particular texts while playing down the significance of others is merely to distort the biblical witness and to demean its very essence.[24] For adherents of this strategy, no hermeneutic can be regarded as satisfactory that does not take into account all parts of Scripture and make allowance for the different emphases encountered in its manifold traditions. Reading the Bible must involve the elucidation of the whole in relation to its parts and its parts in relation to the whole, and the significance of individual statements must be measured in the context of the entire thrust of biblical revelation. This approach demands that Scripture be viewed as a unified, organic entity, and it requires the reader to respect the overarching perspective and character of the tradition in its entirety. Unlike the 'canon-within-a-canon' strategy, this approach does not neglect or sideline the unpalatable parts of Scripture; it merely asserts that some of its more unsavoury aspects will appear less troublesome once account is taken of the broader vision represented by the tradition as a whole.

This strategy has been embraced by some feminist critics as the most effective way of dealing with the biblical texts that are demeaning and disparaging towards women. The presence of such passages in the Hebrew Bible is openly acknowledged, but it is argued that, provided due account is taken of the overall context of Scripture, the patriarchal bias can be counterbalanced with one which is less sexist and discriminatory. Texts which view women negatively should be viewed in the light of others which offer a more positive assessment of their role and contribution; narratives which appear to be imbued with male chauvinistic attitudes should be seen in the context of others which are free of sexist presuppositions.

Supporters of the holistic approach thus try to achieve a sense of proportion in their interpretation of Scripture, and believe that the biblical passages which are favourably disposed towards women may be used as a corrective to other texts that appear to be more oppressive in their outlook. Thus, for example, passages in which women are regarded as the property of their husbands (cf. Ex. 20:17) must be seen in the light of other texts in which they are depicted as possessing a measure of freedom, autonomy and self-respect (Prov. 19:26; 20:20); laws in which women are discriminated against must be viewed against injunctions which resolutely uphold their dignity and status (cf. Ex. 20:12; 21:15, 17; Deut. 5:16); narratives which depict the meekness and self-abnegation of women (Judg. 11:34–40) must be set in the context of stories which view them as courageous, resourceful and strong-willed (Num. 12:1–2; 1 Kgs 21:1–16); passages which appear to limit the role of women to the domestic realm must be seen in the light of texts which suggest that they could take an active part in commercial transactions and could participate freely in public affairs (Prov. 31:10–31).

The presence of such counter-passages in Scripture suggests that the Hebrew Bible is far from presenting a rigidly uniform perspective concerning the status and role of women, and that it contains positive affirmations that can be used to challenge, correct or transcend the dominant patriarchal ethos. According to the holistic approach, therefore, passages in the Hebrew Bible that seem objectionable and offensive to women are problematic only when viewed in isolation; once the broader, canonical context of Scripture is taken into account, the biblical text is not as irredeemably patriarchal and sexist as is often supposed.

Among feminist biblical scholars, such an approach has most cogently been advocated by Phyllis Bird (1974, pp.41–88), who has argued that due regard must be given to the full range of evidence presented in the Hebrew Bible concerning the role and status of women. According to Bird, feminist critics should studiously avoid an obsessive concentration on isolated texts and should seek, instead, to do justice to the variety of viewpoints represented in Scripture. Individual images of women must be evaluated in the context of the testimony of the Hebrew Bible as a whole, for the meaning and significance of isolated passages may be changed or modified once reference is made to the broader sweep of biblical testimony. Thus, for example, to focus exclusively on the subordinate role of women implied in Gen. 2 may give a false or misleading impression of the status generally accorded to women in Scripture, and in order to avoid any such misconception, an attempt must be made 'to locate the creation accounts within the larger testimony of the Old Testament'.[25] Bird thus proceeds to examine the role of women in the legal, didactic, historical and prophetic writings, and concludes that, when viewed in this broader context, the attitude exhibited towards women in the Hebrew Bible is not as negative or hostile as is often assumed.[26] Bird does not, of course, deny that there are many biblical texts which are blatantly discriminatory and in which women are clearly relegated to an inferior position; her concern, however, is to emphasize that such texts are not necessarily representative, since they 'do not describe all situations or all points of view' (1974, p.71).

It is easy to understand the appeal that the holistic approach might have for feminist critics (and, indeed, for biblical scholars who have no particular feminist axe to grind), for it is a strategy that gives the impression of fullness, completeness and balance. The hermeneutic principle which undergirds it seems perfectly sound and logical: only by recognizing the whole range of biblical testimony, and discovering the general drift of Scripture, are we likely to arrive at sensible, balanced conclusions regarding the role of women in the biblical text. Moreover, such a strategy is in tune with recent trends in biblical research, where the traditional 'atomistic' approach to Scripture is increasingly giving way to studies which focus on large sections of the biblical text, including entire books, whatever the original date and authorship of their individual components. Further, the strategy guards against the danger of evaluating the subject-matter of the Hebrew Bible in a way that is predetermined to be ultimately positive or negative; indeed, it suggests that such a dialectic either/or approach to Scripture is overly simplistic, for to view the biblical teaching as either oppressive and restrictive or as liberating and self-affirming does less than justice to the wide range of evidence available. But perhaps the most important contribution of this approach is its insight that the biblical depiction of gender roles is not as uniform or stereotyped as is frequently assumed. Consequently, there may be an element of truth in its claim that biblical scholars, by failing to take account of the variety of viewpoints represented in the Hebrew Bible, have managed to make the book far more sexist and discriminatory than it actually is.

However, the strategy is not without its potential drawbacks. By its seeking to do justice to the entire panoply of voices heard within Scripture, there is a danger that the specificity of each voice in its context will be muted, and that the tensions, fractures and gaps in the text, which often prove to be most illuminating, will be overlooked. But the main problem with the holistic approach centres on its practical implementation, for the task of recovering the totality of the biblical message in order to do justice to its parts is not one which the ordinary reader of Scripture can easily undertake. While one may well agree that, in principle, the Bible must be allowed to speak for itself in the full range and variety of its teachings, the process of discerning the 'main thrust' or 'general drift' of Scripture is not as simple as adherents of this strategy would like to suppose. The fact is that when people read the Bible they do not normally contemplate the existence of multiple witnesses within the canon, and still less do they pause to ponder on the nature of their relation to one another. Reading the Bible with an eye to its wholeness is a perfectly laudable aim, but it is a task which is easier said than done.

The fact is that, even if we were to give due regard to the testimony of Scripture as a whole rather than to its individual witnesses, it is likely that we would still conclude that it is a predominantly male document which reflects a deeply rooted conviction regarding women's social and legal inferiority. In other words, were we to be asked, 'Is the Bible *as a whole* vulnerable to the charge of sexism?' we would surely be hard pressed to answer in the negative with a clear conscience.

Conclusion

It is important to recognize that the strategies discussed above are not necessarily mutually exclusive, for some feminists favour using more than one methodological approach, while others adopt different approaches on different occasions, depending upon the text to be analysed. What is clear, however, is that there is no single monolithic feminist approach to Scripture;[27] rather, feminist scholars have addressed the issue of the inferior role of women in the Bible in various ways, ranging from the 'reformist' to the revolutionary, from the conservative to the radical, and have done so with varying degrees of success. As we have seen, some have reacted strongly against its overwhelmingly masculine bias, arguing that the roots of sexism are so deeply embedded within the Judaeo-Christian traditions that their removal must entail the loss of the religious traditions themselves; others, more appeasing in their approach, and understandably reticent to relinquish their biblical heritage, have sought to exonerate the Bible of the charge of sexism and have even explored ways in which it may be used as a weapon in the struggle for female emancipation. Such diversity has usually been welcomed by feminist critics, who have argued that each method has its own distinctive contribution to make to the transformation of patriarchal culture.[28]

But although some of the strategies outlined in this chapter have yielded potentially valuable results, the methodological perspectives which have been analysed have their limitations. The view taken in this volume is that the most fruitful contributions have come from feminist critics who have adopted a literary rather than historical approach to the biblical text.[29] The door to a feminist literary approach to the Bible was opened by Phyllis Trible, whose volume *God and the Rhetoric of Sexuality* (1978) invited serious and sustained reflection on the rhetoric of the biblical text and the literary structure of individual passages. But while the volume provided many illuminating insights concerning the literary representations of women in the Hebrew Bible, it was almost exclusively text-oriented, and comparatively little account was taken of the impact such texts might have on the individual reader. This deficiency was remedied in Trible's later volume, *Texts of Terror*, where she attempted to consider the writer, reader and text 'in a collage of understanding' (1984, p.1). It is this reader-oriented approach to the patriarchal texts of the Hebrew Bible that will be explored in the present volume. Our aim will be to examine the ways in which the biblical authors have contrived to manipulate the reader to accept their own patriarchal agenda, and to suggest how such manipulation should be resisted. Of particular concern, therefore, will be the interconnection between the literary and ideological aspects of the biblical representation of women. In this regard the so-called 'reader-response' theory in literary criticism will prove particularly helpful, and in the next chapter we will examine how this reader-oriented approach has been appropriated by some feminist biblical critics, and how it poses a challenge to some of the established principles of traditional biblical criticism.

Notes

1   Over a hundred years ago, Frances Willard, for example, sought to defend the biblical teaching concerning women on the grounds that scholars had not in the past 'sufficiently recognized the progressive quality of its revelation' (quoted by Schüssler Fiorenza, 1984, p.56).

2   Solomon was notorious in this regard (cf. 1 Kgs 11:3), and David is reported to have had a number of wives (Michal, Abigail, Ahinoam, Bathsheba; cf. 2 Sam. 5:13). Judg. 8:30 suggests that polygamy was taken for granted in the domestic arrangements of early Israel. Cf. de Vaux (1965, pp.24–6).

3   The volume was originally published in French in 1967 under the title, *La Promotion de La Femme Dans La Bible* (Tournai: Casterman).

4   Maertens (1969, pp.149–55). The positive teaching of Jesus concerning the role and status of women is also emphasized by Stagg and Stagg (1978, pp.101–60).

5   Bird (1987, p.404); cf. Hackett (1985, pp.15–38).

6   Cf. Brenner (1985, pp.129–31). In 1 Cor. 11:2–16, Paul insists that women must worship with their heads covered (a clear sign of their subordination), and he appeals to the creation account of Gen. 2 to justify the hierarchy in which God is regarded as the head of Christ, Christ the head of man, and man the head of woman (v.3). Further, he declares that a woman should be obedient to her husband and remain silent in public, and if she wishes to understand community affairs or spiritual matters she should receive instruction from him (1 Cor. 14:34–5; Col. 3:18). Attempts to put a positive gloss on such statements (for example, Stagg and Stagg, 1978, pp.175–9) have usually resulted in the most questionable exegesis of the text; similarly, attempts to argue that the more objectionable passages are the work of later editors, rather than of Paul himself (cf. Scroggs, 1972, pp.283–303) have not proved particularly convincing.

7   Cf. Ruether (1982, p.57). The 'domestic codes', or *Haustafeln*, are thought to be reflected in Col. 3:18–4:1; Ephes. 5:22–6:9; 1 Tim. 2:8–15; 6:1–2; Titus 2:1–10; 1 Pet. 2:13–3:7.

8   Cady Stanton (1898, p.113). A similar view is expressed by Fewell and Gunn, who comment that the 'New Testament is rife with the fruits of patriarchy no less than Genesis–Kings' (1993, p.20).

9   On the theory of 'cultural relativism', see Benedict (1934) and Herskovits (1972).

10 For a discussion of the influence of patriarchy upon the world of ancient Israel and upon the neighbouring cultures of the ancient Near East at the time, see Lerner (1986, pp.54–160).

11 Cf. Meyers (1988, p.29). So, also, Otwell (1977, pp.49–50). Plaskow observes that even today Jews still emphasize the importance of the role of the mother in Israel's survival; living constantly in the fear of war, and concerned at the threat posed to the state of Israel by a growing Palestinian population, they view procreation as woman's most important contribution to Israel's future (1990, p.112).

12 Meyers criticizes scholars who use 'contemporary feminist standards ... to measure the cultural patterns of an ancient society struggling to establish its viability under circumstances radically different from contemporary western conditions' (1988, p.26).

13 Cady Stanton (1895, pp.126–7). Stanton simply could not fathom why 'the customs and opinions of this ignorant people, who lived centuries ago, [should] have any influence in the religious thought of this generation' (p.71).

14 The views advocated in her volume *The Church and the Second Sex* (1968) reflect those of the earlier 'reformist' Daly, as opposed to the post-Christian radical feminist

represented in *Beyond God the Father*. For a similar post-Christian feminist approach to the Bible, see Hampson (1985, pp.341–50; 1990, *passim*). Cf. also Milne (1995, pp.47–73).

15 Speculating on the probable length of a 'depatriarchalized' Bible, Daly ventured to suggest that there might be 'enough salvageable material to comprise an interesting pamphlet' (Daly, 1973, p.205, n.5; cf. Loades, 1991, p.121; 1998, pp.81–2).

16 Cf. Trible (1973, pp.31–4; 1978, pp.22–3, 31–59). A significant proportion of the passages in which God is described as having female attributes is found in the Book of Isaiah; cf. Sawyer (1996, pp.198–219), Gruber (1983, pp.351–9). On the concept of God as mother in Hosea, see Schüngel-Straumann (1986, pp.119–34).

17 For a discussion of the biblical traditions relating to Miriam, see below, pp.65–6, 86–7.

18 The fact that Huldah was consulted in preference to her contemporary, Jeremiah, is regarded as particularly significant, since it serves to further underline her importance and political influence. The Mishnah clearly felt the need to justify her intervention by suggesting that Huldah may have been related (through her husband) to Joshua, the implication being that her pedigree was sufficiently illustrious for the task which she was asked to undertake. See Brenner (1985, pp.59–60).

19 Schüssler Fiorenza (1984, p.13). Ironically, Trible (1985, p.149) contends that Schüssler Fiorenza's own approach is an example of the 'canon-within-a-canon' strategy, since she argues that only the non-sexist and non-androcentric traditions of the Bible have revelatory power.

20 Cf. Fuchs (2000, pp.88, 108). Trible (1978, pp.191–3) concedes that in chapter 4 Ruth is viewed as a vessel for male progeny, but she argues that the patriarchal emphasis of this chapter is alien to the rest of the book. It is doubtful, however, whether such a distinction should be drawn between Ruth 4 and the chapters which precede it. Certainly, Naomi's concern throughout is with patrilineal continuity and, as Fewell has observed, her failure to admit that a daughter-in-law who loves her is better than seven sons (Ruth 4:15) shows her to be 'completely entrenched in patriarchal ideology' (1987, p.82).

21 Cf. Pardes (1992, pp.126–33). Referring to Trible's interpretation of the Song of Songs as love poetry which suggests a return to an Edenic paradise (1978, pp.144–65), Fewell observes that the 'poetic garden of equity, intimacy, and mutuality is not without its thorns' (1987, p.80).

22 For example, Trible's argument that the maternal metaphors for God bear witness to his 'compassionate, merciful, and loving' character (1978, p.39) may simply serve to perpetuate the stereotyping of gender roles that most feminists are anxious to avoid.

23 Among feminist scholars who have questioned the value of plucking positive images out of predominantly androcentric texts, mention may be made of Exum (1994, p.76) and Schüssler Fiorenza (1983, p.21).

24 As Clines (1990a, pp.292–3) notes, the 'holistic' approach (though the actual term 'holistic' is not commonly used even by practitioners of this strategy) is a convenient label 'for a number of quite different interpretational strategies which have in common their opposition to what they see as the fragmentation of the work by other scholarly approaches'. Clines' own volume on the Pentateuch (1978) provides a good example of this type of approach as applied to the first five books of the Hebrew Bible.

25 Bird (1974, p.46). A similar point is made by Pardes (1992, pp.55–8), who argues that the Priestly view of the equality of the sexes in Gen. 1:27 takes on a somewhat different complexion when read in the context of the other Priestly traditions contained in Gen. 1–11, which seem far less favourably disposed to women; similarly, when the Yahwistic traditions in Gen. 1–11 are taken into account, the Yahwist's view of women appears more pro-egalitarian than Gen. 2:21–3 might imply.

26 Bird even goes so far as to suggest that in some biblical passages the female is depicted 'as possessing a measure of freedom, initiative, power and respect that contemporary American women might well envy' (1974, p.42).

27   Cf. Schüssler Fiorenza, who observes that there exists 'not one feminist theology or *the* feminist theology but many different expressions and articulations of feminist theology' (1984, p.3).
28   As Christ and Plaskow have observed, patriarchy is 'a many-headed monster, and it must therefore be attacked with all the strategies at our command' (1979, p.15).
29   Some of the most notable feminist biblical critics, such as Mieke Bal (1987; 1988a; 1988b), have come from a background in secular literary criticism.

Chapter 3

Feminist Criticism and Reader-response Criticism

Feminist biblical scholars have long emphasized the importance of adopting an interdisciplinary approach to the Hebrew Bible and, as was suggested in the previous chapter, some of the most exciting and innovative contributions in recent feminist biblical criticism have come from those who have embraced a reader-response approach to the text. During the heyday of the reader-response movement the issue of gender was seldom explicitly addressed, and it took some time for feminist criticism and reader-response criticism to engage with one another in a serious and sustained way. However, once the link between the disciplines was firmly established, the marriage proved to be fruitful and productive. When feminist biblical critics applied this approach to their reading of the Hebrew Bible, it opened up new avenues in biblical research and served to challenge some of the established principles of traditional biblical scholarship.

The Rise of Reader-response Criticism

In literary theory, the phenomenon known as 'reader-response criticism' emerged as a reaction to the views of the so-called 'New Critics' who flourished in the 1940s and 1950s.[1] The New Critics (or the 'formalists' as they were sometimes called) had emphasized that each literary work was to be regarded as an autonomous, self-sufficient entity, which was to be studied in its own terms, without reference to its cultural and historical context and without regard to the intention of its author or the response of its reader. Meaning was something which inhered exclusively in the text itself, and any extraneous factors were to be discounted, for they would only lead the interpreter astray. The duty of the reader was to come as close as possible to the meaning embedded in the text. Thus, knowledge of the text's production, or of the author's purpose in writing, even if they could be recovered, were irrelevant, for once the literary work had been composed it led a life completely independent of its author. The matter was stated very succinctly by W.K. Wimsatt and M. Beardsley in their seminal essay, 'The Intentional Fallacy', which is sometimes regarded as the New Critics' manifesto: 'The poem is not the critic's own and not the author's (it is detached from the author at birth and goes about the world beyond his power ... to control it)'

(1946, p.470). It was a 'fallacy' to believe that the meaning of a literary composition should correspond to the author's intention; on the contrary, once authors had composed their text, they no longer had any control over how it was to be interpreted and they themselves could claim no special prerogative of understanding their work by virtue of having composed it.[2] According to the New Critics, therefore, any attempt to determine the author's aims and purpose in writing was merely a distraction, for the text was considered to be a free-standing and self-sustaining entity and was regarded as the repository of its own meaning. Every interpretation of a text must therefore find its authentication in the text itself, and not in any extrinsic factors which might be thought to lie behind it.

By abstracting the text from its author and isolating it from its cultural and historical context, the New Critics were able to focus entirely on the literary composition itself. The result of such an approach was inevitably an increased attention to the 'words on the page' and a call for a scrupulously 'close reading' of the text, for only thus could the literary work be broached in a neutral fashion and an attempt be made to determine its definitive meaning.[3] 'Objectivity' was the keynote of the New Critical enterprise, and it was emphasized that there was no place in literary interpretation for subjective impressions or personal intuitions. Only when such intuitive factors had firmly been set to one side could the critic properly begin to analyse the content and structure of the literary text and examine the rich complexity of its meaning. That meaning was regarded as timeless, unchanging and universal; what the text means now is what it had always meant, and the task which faced its readers was to discover, to the best of their ability, what that meaning was.

The text-centred approach of the New Critics, however, gradually came to be viewed as grossly inadequate, for there was an increasing awareness that literary compositions could not be hermetically sealed off from history and isolated from the cultural context in which they were written. Nor, indeed, could they be studied in isolation from their readers. The role of the reader could not simply be marginalized or ignored, for readers were active participants in the determination of literary meaning and creative contributors to the interpretative process. Literary compositions should not be prised away from their contexts of meaning and response, for texts meant what they meant to particular people at particular times and in particular circumstances. The subject (reader) and the object (text) were indivisibly bound together, and the relationship between them was a dynamic process, for texts only became alive and meaningful when people became involved with them and responded to them.

This new approach, which appropriately enough came to be known as 'reader-response criticism', clearly represented a radical departure from the type of methodology advocated by the New Critics.[4] Whereas the latter had exalted the text over both author and reader, the reader-response critics sought to challenge the privileged status of the text and emphasize instead the role of the reader and the profound significance of the reading experience. Whereas the New Critics had dismissed the reader's response as subjective and hopelessly relativistic, the reader-response critics argued that the interplay between text and reader was of considerable significance for the interpretation of a literary work.

This interplay was particularly emphasized by Wolfgang Iser, who was one of the leading advocates of the reader-response approach.[5] Iser argued that the reader must take into account 'not only the actual text but also, and in equal measure, the actions involved in responding to that text' (1972, p.279). Such actions were determined, in large measure, by the literary text itself, for the text was usually full of gaps and indeterminacies, and it was precisely these gaps that activated readers' faculties and stimulated their creative participation. The reader was invited to engage with the text by filling in the blanks and inferring that which the text had withheld (1978, pp.167–72). What a text contained was not 'meaning' as such, but a set of directions enabling the reader to assemble a meaning, directions which each individual would carry out in his or her own way. Reading was a process of anticipation and retrospection which involved the deciphering of words and sentences, the relating of parts to the whole, the modifying of perspectives, the revising of assumptions, the readjustment of perceptions, the asking of questions and the supplying of answers (Iser, 1972, pp.292–4). Instead of looking *behind* the text for the meaning, the meaning was to be found *in front of* the text, in the active participation of the reader (Iser, 1980, pp.106–19). Such participation was vital, according to Iser, for by itself the text was just an inert object, a lifeless assemblage of paper, binding and print. The role of the reader was to bring that text to life and, in the words of Norman Holland, to play 'the part of a prince to the sleeping beauty' (1975, p.12).

In a similar vein, the American critic Stanley Fish (another leading figure in the reader-response movement) argued that the object of critical attention should be the experience of the reader rather than any objective structures or patterns in the text itself (Fish, 1980). Far from playing a passive, submissive role, readers were active agents in the making of meaning and were encouraged to reflect upon the impact which the literary work had had upon them.[6] According to Fish, the literary text was not so much an object to be analysed as an effect to be experienced. Consequently, the fundamental question that should be asked of any text was not 'What does it mean?' but 'What does it *do*?', and the task of the critic was to analyse '*the developing responses of the reader in relation to the words as they succeed one another in time*' (1972, pp.387–8). Understood in this way, the act of reading involved far more than a perception of what was written; it was rather to be regarded as a dynamic process, an activity, an 'event'.[7]

One of the effects of such an approach, of course, was to undermine all belief in the objectivity of the autonomous text; instead, emphasis came to be placed on the indeterminacy of each text's meaning. Since the reader was called upon to co-operate with the text in the production of meaning, and since each text would be actualized by different readers in different ways, allowance had to be made for a broad spectrum of possible readings of the same text. The view cherished by the New Critics that a text contained a single, definitive, authoritative meaning, accessible to all and sundry and wholly resistant to historical change, was abandoned, and texts were made to speak what the reader of the moment wanted them to say.

Of course, the reader-response critics were only too aware that, once the burden of meaning was placed upon the reader, the door would inevitably be flung open to a plurality of divergent – and perhaps even conflicting – interpretations. But this was not generally regarded as a problem; on the contrary, the vast range of possible interpretations merely testified to the text's richness and inexhaustibility. Indeed, this was what made literary texts worthy of the name. Unlike legal statutes, where a single, agreed interpretation was required, and where there was only one generally accepted understanding of the text, literature thrived on subjective perceptions, and the more interpretations it attracted, the more profound the text appeared to be.[8] Consequently, different readings of literary texts were not merely tolerated but positively encouraged; rival voices were not simply permitted but actively cultivated. The reader-response critics were thus happy to promote the idea that texts were capable of producing an infinite variety of diverse readings and they saw no need to adjudicate between them, for all readings had equal validity and could be regarded as equally legitimate. There was therefore no need to be in the least embarrassed by differing interpretations of the same text; on the contrary, they were to be welcomed, for the response of the reader to the text was at least as interesting, if not more so, than the content of the text itself.

The Feminist Challenge to Biblical Scholarship

Such developments in modern literary theory inevitably raised questions concerning the way in which the Hebrew Bible should be interpreted, and feminist critics were in the vanguard of those who used the insights of reader-response criticism to debunk some of the most cherished ideals of established biblical scholarship.

One such ideal to which biblical scholars had traditionally aspired was that of neutral, dispassionate, value-free scholarship. Their task, as they saw it, was to broach the text as objectively as possible and apply all the methodological tools at their disposal in order to ensure that their exposition was free from misguided assumptions and personal prejudices. Only by cultivating a neutral stance towards their subject matter could they be sure that their own beliefs and theological preconceptions did not cloud their judgment and colour their interpretation. Subjectivity was regarded as the curse of biblical scholarship, for it only led to a distortion of the text by interpreters who manipulated it to mean whatever they wanted it to say. Interpretations such as those offered by feminist critics and liberation theologians were inevitably viewed with a measure of suspicion, for such scholars had clearly abandoned all pretensions to objectivity and were obviously intent upon reading the Bible with their own interests at heart and their own agendas to promote. Biblical scholars in the more traditional mould, on the other hand, could congratulate themselves that their own reading of the Bible was thankfully free of such ideological distortions. By practising the canons of biblical criticism, they had presented what they believed to be the 'true' meaning of the text and had proffered what they hoped might be its definitive interpretation.

Feminist critics, however, regarded such an approach to the biblical text as misguided and as a sign of the failure of biblical scholars to avail themselves of the insights of contemporary literary criticism. In the first place, they questioned the wisdom of attempting to seek out the definitive meaning of a biblical text. In fact, they argued that scholars who purported to offer such a reading were doing the discipline a disservice, for they were, in effect, closing off other possible interpretations in the interests of privileging their own. Such monolithic readings of the Bible were flatly rejected by feminist scholars in favour of the view that biblical texts were open to a plurality of legitimate interpretations. Indeed, the possibility that the same text was capable of generating a wide variety of interpretations was part of the fascination of studying Scripture and was what made the Bible 'a garden of delight to the exegete' (Ostriker, 1993, p.62). There was therefore no attempt by feminist scholars to claim exclusivity for the readings which they presented; indeed, such claims were openly derided, for they smacked of the very authoritarianism in biblical scholarship that they were anxious to avoid. Instead of trying to discover the 'original', 'correct' or 'definitive' meaning of the text, they were far more concerned to present a spectrum of possible alternative readings. Texts, by their very nature, triggered different interpretations; they were, in the words of Mieke Bal, 'the occasion of a reaction' (1987, p.132), and it was inevitable that readers would react to a text in a number of different, perhaps even conflicting, ways.

Further, feminist critics cast doubt on the objective, neutral posturing of traditional biblical scholarship, regarding it as one of the outmoded legacies of the Enlightenment ideal of dispassionate, disinterested inquiry (Schüssler Fiorenza, 1988, pp.10–11). They argued that even the most aggressively 'neutral' scholars could not expound the biblical text without some degree of involvement, for their own interests and experiences would inevitably determine – or, at least, influence – their interpretation. The biblical exegete was not a blank sheet on which the text of Scripture would mechanically inscribe its own meaning; rather, one's efforts at interpretation were always filtered through one's own prior social, cultural, political and ideological categories. Subjective readings were by no means confined to feminist or other minority groups, for all readers were, in their own ways, 'interested parties' (Clines, 1995), with their own axe to grind, their own vested interests to promote, and their own points of view to defend.

For feminist critics, such subjectivity was particularly evident in the male bias of much traditional biblical scholarship. Such bias was seldom openly acknowledged and yet it often had a profound and far-reaching effect upon the way in which the biblical text was interpreted. Interpretations which claimed to be objective and dispassionate were usually nothing of the kind, for they reflected the male values and male perspectives of the individual interpreter. Biblical texts concerning women were often either misunderstood or ignored by male commentators, and there was a notable tendency on their part to re-inscribe (albeit unconsciously) the patriarchal ideology of the biblical authors. Feminist critics therefore called for a new critical self-awareness on the part of biblical interpreters, and urged them to resist the 'male-centred phallacy of objective and ultimate truth' (Fuchs, 2000, p.27).

But biblical exegetes were challenged not only to cast off the mantle of objectivity, but to question and critique the text which was being interpreted. If its content proved contentious or unethical, it was their duty to express their disapproval and articulate their opposition to the biblical teaching. Instead of being enthralled to a reverent reading of Scripture, they were encouraged to become 'dissenting readers'.

The Dissenting Reader

In modern literary theory, the term 'reader-response criticism' refers to a diverse assortment of methodological perspectives, and the spectrum of reader-response critics is so broad that it is questionable whether they should all be categorized under a single, neat heading.[9] Indeed, if we were to ask reader-response critics the ostensibly simple question, 'Who is the reader?' it is likely that we would be provided with a confusingly large number of answers, for over the years the discipline has developed a rich panoply of different types of reader. These have been defined and categorized in various ways, and include, for example, the 'implied reader' (Iser, Booth), the 'model reader' (Eco), the 'ideal reader' (Culler), the 'informed reader' (Fish) and the 'actual reader' (Jauss), to name but a few.[10] The type of reader with which the present volume is concerned, and which seems most relevant to a feminist critical approach to the Hebrew Bible, is the 'dissenting reader' or – to use the phrase coined by Judith Fetterley – the 'resisting reader'.

Fetterley's study of the 'resisting reader' was published in 1978 and is now commonly regarded as a classic of feminist reader-response criticism. The aim of her study was to examine the problem encountered by the female reader reading male-oriented works of American literary fiction. Fetterley argued that the canon of classical American literature was thoroughly androcentric; it was written from a male perspective, imbued with male presuppositions and intended for a male-implied audience. Women who read this literature were thus conditioned to think as men, to embrace a male point of view, and accept as normal and legitimate a male system of values (1978, pp.xii, xx). Fetterley referred to this as a process of 'immasculation'. One factor which perpetuated such immasculation in American literature was the ubiquitous use of the personal pronoun 'he' and the noun 'man' to include both sexes, for this had the invidious psychological effect of making the female appear invisible. This process of immasculation was a powerful instrument of sexual politics (though it had rarely been recognized as such) for it demanded that women participate in an experience from which they were excluded, and it required them to identify against themselves. The text solicited their complicity with its patriarchal ideology and persuaded them to view the male perspective as universal and the male experience as the norm.

The goal of the feminist critic, according to Fetterley, was to disrupt this process of immasculation by drawing attention to issues such as identity, gender and power relations, and by making readers more conscious of their reading experience and the subtle ways in which the text sought to manipulate their response. Without such awareness the female reader might find herself embracing the patriarchal ethos presupposed in the text and giving an automatic nod of assent to the androcentric values of its author. Female readers could not simply refuse to read such patriarchal texts, for the dominant literary and critical traditions were almost entirely male-oriented; they could, however, adopt a strategy of resistance and refuse to accept the assumptions and values promoted by the author. The very act of reading thus needed to be reassessed and redefined. Encounter with the text required not passive consumption but judicious and sceptical questioning. It meant reading 'against the grain' of the text and adopting an adversarial attitude towards the written word. Of course, becoming a 'resisting reader' was by no means easy, for there was a natural predisposition on the part of women to adopt the male viewpoint; indeed, this was part and parcel of the strategy of reading learned in the course of acquiring literacy. Yet such an adversarial strategy was necessary if women were to exorcize 'the male mind that has been implanted in us' (Fetterley, 1978, p.xxii).

Now, in many respects, Fetterley's observations are relevant for female readers of the Hebrew Bible, for they, too, are faced with texts written predominantly, if not entirely, by male authors. It is true that some scholars have claimed to have found evidence of female authorship in the biblical writings,[11] but even if it could be demonstrated that particular books or particular traditions within the Hebrew Bible were composed by women, the fact remains that it is the male world-view that finds expression in the biblical text, while the female perspective is muted if not altogether excluded (cf. Exum, 1993, p.10). Female readers of Scripture are faced with an androcentric canon and, like female readers of classical American fiction, they are invited to participate in an experience from which they themselves

are often excluded. The male-dominated language of the Bible has the effect
of making them feel invisible by subsuming them under masculine linguistic
terms.[12] Reference has already been made to the fact that the Decalogue (as
regards both grammar and substance) addresses the community only as the
male heads of households (see above, p.1). Although its injunctions are
widely regarded as indispensable for the survival of human communities, it
is only the male 'you' that is addressed by its commands; women are absent,
or, at best, 'sub-indexed as male' (Brenner, 1994b, p.255). Moreover, the
context in which the Decalogue was mediated to the people (Ex.
19:1–20:21) confirms the absence of women at this crucial juncture of
Israel's history. When the Israelites stand at Sinai ready to receive the
covenant, the men are commanded not to 'go near a woman' for three days
(Ex. 19:15), the implication being that they were to refrain from sexual
relations prior to the theophany at the holy mountain.

According to Judith Plaskow, nowhere is the exclusion of women in the
Hebrew Bible more apparent than in this narrative, for it suggests that it was
only the male members of the community whose ritual purity had to be
protected and that it was they alone who were to be the recipients of the
divine communication (1990, pp.25–7; cf. Brenner, 1994b, p.256). The
narrative is regarded as particularly significant by feminist biblical critics,
for it appears to set forth a pattern to be repeated time and time again in the
Hebrew Bible in which women were excluded both from the central
institutions of Israel's faith and from full membership of the covenant
community.

Further, the basic symbols of biblical faith – king, lord, master, father and
husband – occur with such frequency in the Hebrew Bible that the female
reader almost inevitably finds herself internalizing such images and
identifying with the male perspective (cf. Schüssler Fiorenza, 1998, p.87).
In this regard, reading the text of Scripture, like reading the canon of
classical American literature, may be said to involve a process of
'immasculation'; indeed, the Bible has been described by one leading
feminist biblical critic as 'one of the most paradigmatic immasculating texts
of Western culture' (Fuchs, 2000, p.19). It encourages women to suppress
their own identity and to see the world 'with male chauvinist eyes' (Daly,
1973, p.49). But in the process of identifying with the masculine images of
the text, the female reader is often compelled to identify against herself. For
example, when the prophets use the marriage metaphor to depict the
relationship between Yahweh and Israel, the apostate nation is always
identified with the unfaithful wife, while God is regularly portrayed as the
faithful, long-suffering husband. It is the wife who has prostituted herself by
going after other lovers while the husband has done everything in his power
to prevent her and to plead with her to return (cf. Hos. 2:2–23). Now the
rhetorical strategy of the biblical text is clear: readers (both male and
female) are expected to empathize with the male-identified deity and to ally
themselves with the male point of view. So powerful and so subtle is the

prophetic propaganda that the reader unconsciously internalizes its message and embraces its ideology (see below, pp.50–52). Yet, in doing so, the female reader is seduced into reading against her own interests, for she is made to concur with the prophet's view of the woman as the unfaithful and unreliable partner, and in doing so she allows her own sex to bear the burden of guilt for the breakdown of the marriage relationship (cf. Exum, 2000, p.99).

Now, for many feminist biblical critics, the most effective way to counter such patriarchal indoctrination is by adopting the method advocated by Fetterley, namely, by assuming an adversarial attitude towards the biblical text. Only by reading against its androcentric grain can readers hope to break the text's ideological hold over them. Reading 'against the grain' does not, of course, mean rejecting the text in its entirety; on the contrary, feminist critics are prepared to accept much of the 'objective' information provided by the omniscient narrator as reliable and authoritative. What they will not accept, however, is the narrator's interpretation of his characters' motives or the value judgments which he passes upon their actions (whether these are explicitly stated or merely implied). The biblical author will naturally try to persuade the reader to accept his evaluation of a particular character, but feminist critics have learnt to distrust that evaluation, being only too aware that the narrative might just be a vehicle for the male author to pass off his own personal prejudices. Feminist critics are only too aware that the biblical narrator wields rhetorical control over the story which he relates, but they steadfastly refuse to be manipulated by the text. Instead of docilely accepting the value judgments of the biblical author, they engage in a critical appraisal of the text's ideology and read the Bible against its patriarchal framework. For them, reading involves what Harold Bloom has called the 'art of defensive warfare' (1975, p.126) and feminist critics identify the war in which they are engaged as a struggle against patriarchy.

One feminist biblical critic who has effectively deployed such a strategy of resistance is Mieke Bal, whose reading of the Book of Judges deliberately focuses on the insignificant, the trivial, the different – the very elements which the traditional, dominant readings have tended to suppress or exclude. She attempts to change the perspective of the text and reverse the established priorities in its interpretation so that 'what is seen to be central will be marginalized, and what has been treated as marginal will become central' (1988a, p.2). Bal adopts what she calls a strategy of 'countercoherence': the more something is repressed in the text, the more it needs to be highlighted; the more it is hidden by the author, the more it needs to be brought to the surface. In other words, she conceives her task as being to expose the very elements which the male author wanted to suppress. The text of the Book of Judges, for example, gives the leading part to men, so Bal begins by focusing on the women; the biblical authors concentrate upon the heroes, so Bal dwells upon the victims; the narratives preserve the anonymity of the female figures, so Bal proceeds to give them a name (1988a, p.17; 1990, p.19).

Other feminist scholars have applied a similar strategy to stories outside the Book of Judges by attempting to recover the submerged strains of women's voices in the patriarchal text, and to view events from their perspective. For example, what if the story of Abraham were told from the point of view of Sarah, whose sexuality was pawned on account of Abraham's cowardice, or from the point of view of Hagar, who, having been enslaved and afflicted is commanded by God to return and submit to further affliction (Fewell, 1998, pp.182–94)? How would David's adultery with Bathsheba have looked if the story had been told from her perspective rather than his? How would the account of Hosea's marriage have appeared if his supposedly promiscuous wife had been the narrator (Sherwood, 1996, pp.302–21)? The type of methodology deployed by these feminist critics can bear many names – 'ideological critique', 'oppositional criticism', 'reading against the grain', 'a hermeneutic of suspicion' – but its underlying assumption is that the act of reading should involve resistance to the dominant structures of power inscribed in the biblical text.

Such resistance clearly involves a radical departure from the way in which the Bible is customarily read, for traditionally readers have been conditioned to remain slavishly respectful to the text's claims and to respond to its demands with uncritical obeisance. They have regarded themselves as passive recipients of the text, and have felt obliged to submit to its authority and to acquiesce in its value judgments. They have read – and frequently studied – the Hebrew Bible with an untroubled admiration instead of with a restless questioning. The type of approach developed by Fetterley, however, serves to remind readers that they have a duty to converse and interact with the text, and that the Hebrew Bible must be read in an openly critical, and not in a passively receptive, way. As they read Scripture, they must respond as thinking individuals and feel free to make their own judgments and draw their own conclusions regarding the validity of its claims. They may want to criticize its demands, interrogate its values and expose its double standards. They may want to resist texts that appear oppressive or tyrannical, and reject demands that they feel should not (and perhaps cannot) be fulfilled. They may want to argue that the tradition underlying the text is ethically questionable and that to accept the text as it stands is both morally and intellectually indefensible. In brief, they may want to 'read against the grain' of the text and call some of its more dubious pronouncements into account in their own court of ethical judgment.

Of course, there will be times when they will want to respond positively to the text, embracing its demands whole-heartedly in the conviction that its teaching confirms what they intrinsically believe to be right and proper. But what they should not permit themselves is the luxury of a simple, undivided affirmation of the Bible's entire contents. To accept the value statements of the text in utter passivity, without allowing oneself the freedom to reflect critically upon its claims and to question its assumptions is merely to foster a sense of complacency, and to reduce the act of reading the Bible to a stultifying, mind-numbing exercise. The task of the reader, therefore, is to engage in a vigorous dialogue and debate with the Hebrew Bible, resisting statements that appear to be morally objectionable, and taking a critical stance against what he or she may regard as the excesses of the biblical text.

Feminist critics insist that the Bible must be held ethically accountable, if only because of the profound influence, for good or ill, which it has exercised upon its readers. While it is true that it has been appealed to in support of the most worthy causes, it is no less true that it has been unashamedly exploited, at various times and in various places, to legitimate war, to nurture anti-Semitism, to justify slavery and – as feminist critics are quick to point out – to promote misogyny. It is precisely because of the negative ramifications of some of the Bible's teachings that it is the duty of the biblical interpreter to look at the social, ethical and political repercussions of various texts and of various readings of various texts. The challenge that faces the biblical exegete is to apply to the Hebrew Bible the kind of ethical–ideological probings that scholars such as Wayne Booth (1983; 1988), Terry Eagleton (1978) and Hillis Miller (1987) have applied to secular literature. Indeed, it is arguable that the need to subject the Bible to ideological critique is even more pressing than in the case of secular literature, for millions of people have privileged the Bible as a norm by which to live and have submitted themselves to its moral dictates.

It is therefore the duty of the biblical interpreter to ask not simply 'What does the text mean?' but (in the words of Stanley Fish) 'What does the text *do*?' What effect does it have upon its readers? What kind of values does it advocate? Is it doing anyone any harm? Does it advocate hatred and violence? Does it promote racism, misogyny, colonialism, xenophobism or homophobism? Does it contribute to the general well-being of society or does it have a negative, detrimental effect, perhaps by reinforcing the language of oppression and domination? Before such questions can be addressed, however, the biblical interpreter must recognize that the Bible is a profoundly ideological document which not only describes a patriarchal society but which promotes and justifies such a society, regarding it as natural, inevitable and divinely ordained.

The Ideology of the Text

Critics of secular literature have long recognized that very few texts are entirely free of ideological commitment, for whenever people engage in the act of writing they almost invariably do so from a particular standpoint. Even the most seemingly neutral narratives are laced with particular values, presuppositions and ideologies. Sometimes the ideology is clearly manifest in what the text actually says; at other times it is merely suggested by its eloquent silences. But whether the writer (or, for that matter, the reader) is aware of it or not, the literary text is usually a vehicle for expressing a particular ideological viewpoint.

In recent years there has been a growing realization that the text of the Hebrew Bible is similarly coded in ideological terms, and scholars have discerned ideological tendencies in various strands of the biblical tradition.[13] It is now widely regarded as axiomatic that the biblical texts are the expression of a particular world-view, and there is some evidence to suggest that that view is the one seen through the lenses of the patriarchal ruling classes. Far from reporting what ordinary people in ancient Israel thought and believed, the Hebrew Bible appears to reflect the values and aspirations of a privileged male elite.

Many of the laws in the Pentateuch, for example, were clearly designed to encourage and legitimate a system of values that happened to be congenial to the male ruling classes. The numerous slave laws provide an interesting case in point, for such enactments were almost certainly imposed by the rich and powerful by way of ideological control (cf. Ex. 21:2–11; Deut. 15:12–17). They were drafted in such a way as to persuade dependent people that they were extremely fortunate to be living under the protection of their wealthy masters: the slaves had, after all, been provided with meaningful employment and some measure of security, and although they had been deprived of their freedom, their situation was infinitely preferable to that of the debt-ridden land-holders who were at the mercy of exploitative and unscrupulous money-lenders. The clear implication behind such legislation is that slaves should count their blessings and be grateful for being the recipients of such favours.

Naturally, the ideology present in such texts is all the more potent for being concealed. The need for such social stratification within society is presented almost as though it were a self-evident, universally accepted fact of life. The social system is invested with a spurious air of naturalness and inevitability and made to appear as the very essence of common sense and normality. In order to establish and safeguard their position of power, it was necessary to make the slaves accept the social role which was their destiny. The text therefore rationalizes the hierarchical system by providing a logical and credible explanation for its existence. Of course the class system was necessary and just! Of course a society without masters and slaves would be intolerable! How could it be otherwise? By means of such ideological conditioning the oppressed became victims of a kind of myopic vision which prevented them from seeing the essential injustice of their situation. The ideology was presented in such a convincing way that it had the effect of making the slave resigned, indifferent and unable to formulate criticism or even to imagine an alternative system.[14] The captives were thus reduced to a state of passivity, and became persuaded of the justice of the very social order that oppressed them. Moreover, as something of an added safeguard (lest anyone should have the temerity to question the fairness of such a system), the slave laws were presented as decrees issued by God himself, implying that such enactments must be regarded by all as timeless, absolute and authoritative. In this way the legislation pertaining to slaves was made to appear immune to criticism or rational reflection, and the powerful were thus able to forestall any critical interrogation of the status quo.[15]

Now as we read such legal enactments in the Hebrew Bible it is surely relevant to ask: in whose interests were they formulated? What values and priorities were they trying to promote? Whose voice is being privileged in these texts and why? What category of people stood to gain by the enforcement of such laws? (cf. Clines, 1997, pp.21–2). The answer seems clear enough: they were designed to serve the interests of the rich and powerful in ancient Israel and to maintain power in the hands of the ruling classes by keeping people firmly in their appointed places in society.[16] But the laws were formulated in such a way as to highlight the master's compassion and munificence rather than the slave's discomfort and misfortune. It is only when we read between the lines of the laws in question – what the reader-response critics call the gaps and interstices of the text – that we begin to appreciate the ulterior motives that are at work.

The above observations concerning Israel's slave laws are particularly relevant when we come to examine the patriarchal ideology of the Hebrew Bible, for a similar strategy appears to have been deployed to endorse the power relations between the sexes. Here, too, the law proved a potent instrument in enforcing women's subjugation, and, since the law was given by God, the subjugation of women came to be regarded as a divinely sanctioned principle, and the male viewpoint was imperceptibly 'metamorphosed into God's viewpoint' (Daly, 1973, p.47). But patriarchal values were imposed not only, or even primarily, through legislation, but through stories recounting the adventures and exploits of some of the leading figures in the nation's history. Indeed, the biblical narrative tradition was, in many respects, a far more effective instrument of ideological control than legal stipulations, for it was able to present male supremacy and female subordination as a normal, natural and inevitable part of human experience. So subtle and persuasive was its representation of the male/female relationship that it induced women to be resigned to their inferior position and to accept it as part of their nature and destiny. Such ideological manipulation was vital if the patriarchal enterprise was to triumph, for the hierarchical division between male and female could not succeed without the consent of the dominated as well as the dominant sex. This consent was obtained largely through role socialization and gender stereotyping. Men were cast in the role of the nation's heroes and warriors, while women were consigned to the domestic realm, and persuaded that the most important function which they could perform was the production of male offspring. By deft use of images, careful construction of dialogue, and clever and subtle characterization, the biblical narratives sought to legitimize and justify the patriarchal structuring of society, and reinforce its assumptions about the inferiority of women.

Ideological Critique

Feminist critics insist that it is not enough merely to discover the ideological undercurrents of a particular text; the biblical exegete must subject its ideology to critical analysis. This is by no means an easy task, for the ideology is often presented in such a matter-of-fact, that-goes-without-saying way that it does not occur to readers to pause and question its underlying logic and assumptions. The ideology swathes them in the illusion that this is, indeed, the way things should be, and so convincing is its propaganda that they can hardly imagine how things could be different. They thus find themselves taken in by the text's ideology, lulled into a state of passive acceptance and seduced into accepting as valid and legitimate a set of values which, in their more guarded moments, they might reject, or at least question. Of course, it is a tribute to the success of the biblical authors that they have been able to manipulate their readers in such a way, for the job of purveyors of ideology has always been to persuade people to see the world as *they* see it and not as it is in itself.

Such is the power that the biblical text wields over the reader that even biblical scholars who pride themselves on being neutral and disinterested observers often succumb (albeit, perhaps, unconsciously) to the text's ideology and accept it as their own. D.J.A. Clines has perceptively demonstrated how commentators on the book of Amos, for example, have fallen precisely into this trap (1995, pp.76–93). Instead of distancing themselves from the prophetic voice and standing outside the ideology of the text, they have suppressed their critical instincts and found themselves in tacit agreement with the prophet's stance. Amos is a man of God and so (by definition) what he says must be right and true. Thus, when the prophet threatens with exile the self-indulgent who lie on beds of ivory and eat of the choicest meats (Am. 6:4–7), his social analysis is accepted without demur and the threat of deportation is regarded as just and fair. The rich and powerful, claims Amos, have exploited the poor and oppressed the needy and fully deserve to be sent into exile (cf. Am. 4:1–3). And so say all of us. Similarly, when Amos castigates the foreign nations for their antisocial activities and threatens them with destruction and ruin (Am.1:3–2:3), 'high-minded commentators who would not harm a fly themselves suddenly join the hanging and flogging brigade and think no punishment too severe' (1995, p.91).

In brief, the ideology has cast its magic spell over its readers and they are seduced into a readerly identification with Amos' words. Instead of taking a step back from the text and critically questioning its assumptions, they have merged into empathetic harmony with the text's ideology and have all but embraced it as their own. Such is the complicity between the text and its readers that they have automatically conferred unquestioned moral authority upon the prophet and accepted without further thought his own version of the truth. Amos is right, fair and admired for his moral fortitude; his opponents, on the other hand, are wrong, foolish and misguided, and are rightly condemned for their corruption (Clines, 1997, pp.26–7). But what if his opponents were right and he was wrong? Why should we accept only the version of the speaker-in-the-text? What might the situation in Israel during the eighth century BCE have looked like if we had heard it from the lips of Amaziah, the high-priest whom Amos condemns (Am. 7:10–17)? The fact is that everything is heavily stacked in favour of the speaker-in-the-text, whose account of events is seldom questioned and whose claims are rarely resisted (Brenner, 1997c, p.138). Seduced by successive generations of readerly co-operation with the text, scholars have generally been unable to free themselves from its clutches and have shown themselves incapable of rising above the miasma of its ideological smokescreen.

Now one of the merits of the feminist critical approach to the Hebrew Bible is its insistence that commentators should step outside the text's ideology and question its underlying assumptions (Exum, 1993). The manner in which (predominantly male) commentators have been 'taken in' by the ideology of the text is clear from scholarly discussions of Hos. 1–3. Interpreters who have studied the account of Hosea's marriage have traditionally sided automatically with the prophet, so that a 'cosy reciprocity' has been established between the male interpreter and the male-authored text (Sherwood, 1995, p.105). That commentators should find themselves sympathizing with the prophet is not altogether surprising, for the account of the marital breakdown is narrated entirely from the male perspective. It is made abundantly clear that it was the wife who was responsible for the failure of the marriage: she was promiscuous, wayward and obdurate, and had continually played the harlot by going after other lovers (Hos. 2:5, 7). The husband, on the other hand, is depicted as faithful, patient and long-suffering, and although the punishment which he had inflicted upon his wife for her misdemeanour was severe (Hos. 2:1–13), the text implies that it was no more than she deserved for dishonouring her husband in such a fashion. Thus, instead of appearing as the harsh, cruel, vindictive husband, the prophet emerges as the victim in the marriage, and his willingness to take his wife back (instead of divorcing her or having her stoned to death) serves to arouse further sympathy for him as the aggrieved partner. Indeed, so anxious was he to see his wife return that he even enlisted the help of his children to make their mother come to her senses and see the error of her ways (Hos. 2:2). Moreover, the husband's subsequent attempts at reconciliation are so tender, compassionate and heart-rending (Hos. 2:14–23) that the reader is invited to view his previous violent outburst (vv.2–3) as no more than a momentary loss of composure by a man who was so in love that he was prepared to take the most extreme and desperate measures to preserve his marriage intact (cf. Weems, 1995, pp.92–3).

So powerful is the rhetoric of these chapters that the sympathy of the reader (and the biblical commentator) is almost instinctively with the aggrieved husband rather than with the battered wife. The text has deftly manipulated its readers into accepting the prophet's version of events, and coerced them into sharing his righteous indignation at his wife's depraved behaviour. Readers have unconsciously capitulated to the text's ideology and in doing so they have reaffirmed its male perspective and re-inscribed its patriarchal values. As Yvonne Sherwood has observed, such readings of the text have become so commonplace that they have practically acquired a canonical status of their own (1995, p.103).

The problem with such readings, however, is that they fail to apply an ideological critique to the text. While commentators remain captive to the text's ideology they can do little more than repeat its point of view. However, once the exegete looks beyond the male polemic of the text, and refuses to privilege the prophet's word, the marriage of Hosea may be seen in quite a different light. For example, if the prophet was as thoughtful and concerned for his wife's well-being as the text seems to suggest, why did he not stop for a moment to consider whether the breakdown in the marriage relationship might not have been (at least partly) *his* fault? If he was such a good husband and provider, as the text implies, why did his wife abandon him to seek another? Did her actions not suggest that there was some fault or defect in *his* character? Did not the punishment which the prophet threatened to inflict upon his wife (Hos. 2:3–4) suggest that, at the very least, his love was 'as uncompromising and jealous as it was compassionate and tender'? (Weems, 1995, p.31). And, in any case, if she had been taken by the prophet as a wife in order to represent Israel's apostasy (Hos. 1:2), was there not a basic injustice in castigating her for the very behaviour that caused her to be chosen in the first place? (Fontaine, 1995, p.63). These are the kinds of questions asked when the reader refuses to be co-opted by the patriarchal ideology of the text, and when a hearing is given to the silent and suppressed voices within the biblical tradition.[17]

Now it is precisely because biblical scholars – as well as ordinary readers – have allowed themselves to be carried along by the text that ideological critique of the Hebrew Bible is so important. Ideological critique insists that the ideological values of the biblical text must be subjected to critical scrutiny, and that the biblical exegete must learn to apply, as a matter of course, a 'hermeneutic of suspicion' to its content. This involves questioning the text's ideological innocence and exposing those ideologies that so often manifest themselves in reason's garb.

Conclusion

In this chapter we have traced the rise of reader-response criticism in secular literary theory and examined the ways in which feminist biblical critics have availed themselves of the insights of this approach to challenge some of the established principles of biblical scholarship. Of the various types of reader envisaged by the reader-response critics, it was suggested that Judith

Fetterley's 'resisting reader' may prove to be the most helpful for those troubled by the patriarchal bias of the biblical text. By adopting an adversarial reading of the Hebrew Bible and applying a 'hermeneutic of suspicion' to its content, female readers of Scripture will be able to probe, question, challenge and – if necessary – reject its patriarchal assumptions. Such a reading strategy must begin by exposing the ideological undercurrents latent in the biblical tradition, for one of the most effective ways to counter the ideology of patriarchal domination is by drawing attention to the ways in which the text seeks to promote it. The first step, therefore, must be to uncover the literary strategies deployed by the biblical authors to foster their patriarchal agenda, and this will be our aim in the next chapter.

Notes

1　J.C. Ransom published a book in 1941 entitled *The New Criticism*, which seems to have established the term in common usage. Besides Ransom, some of the most important and influential of the New Critics were R. Wellek, Cleanth Brooks, W.K. Wimsatt and M. Beardsley. It is worth noting that their position owed much to the writings of T.S. Eliot (1932) and I.A. Richards (1924). For a discussion of the application of reader-response criticism to biblical studies, see Davies (2003, pp.20–37).

2　Wimsatt argued that 'the design or intention of the author is neither available nor desirable as a standard for judging either the meaning or the value of a work of literary art' (1968, p.222). T.S. Eliot famously refused to comment on the meaning of his own poems, believing that once he had written them he had no special privileges as their interpreter. See Barton (1996, p.148).

3　As Terry Eagleton (1983, p.38) has wryly observed, the use of the expression 'close reading' was somewhat unfortunate, since it seemed to imply 'that every previous school of criticism had read only an average of three words per line'.

4　For exemplary anthologies of the writings of reader-response critics, see Suleiman and Crosman (1980) and Tompkins (1980). Both volumes contain excellent annotated bibliographies.

5　W. Iser's two volumes (1974; 1978) were among the most influential works to emerge from the reader-response critics during the 1970s.

6　One ambiguous aspect of this theory is the extent of the reader's control over the reading experience. Did the text manipulate the reader or did the reader manipulate the text to produce a meaning that suited his or her own interests? In his early reader-oriented criticism (1972) Fish argued that the text manipulates the reader; in his later reincarnation, however, he argued that the reader controls the text (1980). The problem of deciding whether the text (author) or the reader is in charge of the act of reading is a recurrent question in reader-response criticism.

7　Fish, in effect, redefined the meaning of the term 'literary composition' by claiming that it was 'no longer an object, a thing-in-itself, but an *event*, something that *happens* to, and with the participation of, the reader' (1980, p.25).

8　Cf. Morgan and Barton, who comment that 'a thousand interpretations of *Lear* may be enriching, even two of the *Highway Code* disastrous' (1988, p.12).

9　S.R. Suleiman (1980, pp.3–45) subdivides reader-oriented (or, as she prefers to call it, 'audience-oriented') criticism into six major categories: rhetorical; semiotic and structuralist; phenomenological; subjective and psychoanalytic; sociological and historical; and hermeneutic.

10 Other definitions include the 'real' reader, the 'intended' reader, the 'hypothetical' reader, the 'authorial' reader, the 'competent' reader, the 'average' reader. See Fowler (1991, p.26).

11 H. Bloom (1990), for example, suggested that the Yahwist author (the so-called 'J source' in the Pentateuch) may have been a woman, but his hypothesis has generally been regarded as highly speculative (cf. Pardes, 1992, pp.33–7). In a similar vein, Stone (1992, pp.85–99) argued that Deutero-Isaiah was a female prophet, and Hackett (1985, pp.32–3; 1987, pp.160–61) suggested that a corpus of women's literature is preserved in Judg. 3–16, where such heroines as Deborah, Jael and Jephthah's daughter figure prominently. Further, Brenner (1985, pp.46–56) argued that some of the love lyrics in the Song of Songs may have been composed by a woman on account of its use of female imagery and the fact that feminine attributes and emotions are described with such fidelity. See also Dijk-Hemmes (1993b, pp.17–109). The difficulty, however, is in determining adequate criteria according to which female authorship can be demonstrated.

12 Cf. Schüssler Fiorenza (1999, p.60). On the way conventions of grammar constitute a ubiquitous, though often unacknowledged, source of women's oppression, see Spender (1980, pp.7–51).

13 Cf. Amit (1999), Barr (2000), Carroll (1990, pp.309–11), Garbini (1988), Japhet (1997), Jobling (1992), Miller (1976), Pippin (1996), Provan (1995), Sternberg (1985).

14 Habermas argues that ideology serves to 'impede making the foundations of society the object of thought and reflection' (1981, p.166).

15 The Marxist critic F. Jameson uses the expression 'strategy of containment' to refer to an ideology which succeeds in closing off any questioning of a particular situation (1981, pp.52–3).

16 Schüssler Fiorenza notes that the household code traditions of the New Testament were similarly designed to ensure the subordination of slaves, women and children and were formulated in the interests of the male heads of households concerned lest their prerogatives be undermined (1999, p.170).

17 The different perspective which emerges once the interpreter steps outside the ideology of the text is well illustrated in Carole Fontaine's two companion articles on Hosea. In her earlier introductory survey of the prophet (1989, pp.349–58), the marriage metaphor was described in neutral terms and accepted uncritically as a means of representing the relationship between God and his people. In a later article, however, Fontaine conceded that her earlier study had not sufficiently challenged the prevailing scholarly readings of Hosea, and had not satisfactorily critiqued the text's patriarchal assumptions (1995, pp.60–69).

Chapter 4

Unmasking the Text's Ideology

In the previous chapter it was suggested that the most effective way for feminist critics to counter the patriarchal bias of the Hebrew Bible was by reading 'against the grain' of the text and applying a 'hermeneutic of suspicion' to its content. Before this task can be undertaken, however, it is necessary to unmask the patriarchal ideology of the text and to expose its androcentric bias. This is by no means an easy exercise, for texts rarely display their ideological credentials on the surface; on the contrary, the contours of a text's ideology are often concealed, covert and impalpable. Indeed, we may be quite unaware that the text we are reading is ideological, for ideology, in order to be effective, is often cloaked in the garb of disinterested ideas.

The task facing feminist critics, then, is to look beyond the manifest meaning of the biblical narrative in order to root out its unconscious disclosures and to highlight those elements which the text reveals unintentionally. Instead of reading the biblical narrative at face value, they must look behind its ideological scaffolding and try to reveal the author's motives, interests and strategies. How did the biblical narrators conspire to convince women of their inferiority? What literary ploys did they adopt in order to legitimate patriarchal domination? What are their implicit (and explicit) assumptions about gender roles? The aim of the present chapter is to examine some of the literary strategies used by the biblical authors to foster and perpetuate patriarchal values and ideals.

It will be convenient to begin by examining two biblical narratives which deal with the rape of women, for it will be seen that in both cases it is primarily the male world-view that finds expression in the text. Gen. 34 records the rape of Dinah by Shechem and its subsequent repercussions, while 2 Sam. 13 narrates the violation of Tamar by her half-brother, Amnon. These narratives have been chosen because they illustrate how the male authors of the biblical texts deal with a singularly female experience, and how they use the literary devices of plot, dialogue and characterization in the most subtle ways in order to promote their own patriarchal interests.

The Rape of Dinah and Tamar

Gen. 34 is the only narrative in the Hebrew Bible concerned with Jacob's daughter, Dinah. The story records how she left home one day to visit the 'women of the region' (v.1). When Shechem, the son of Hamor, the prince of the region, saw her, he seized her and proceeded to rape her (v.2).[1] Subsequently, however, Shechem found himself drawn to Dinah and expressed a wish to marry her (vv.3–4). Negotiations ensued between Hamor and Jacob's sons, and the latter agreed to the marriage of their sister on condition that Shechem's tribe became 'as we are and every male among you be circumcised' (v.15). The Shechemites fulfilled this condition, but while they were in the process of circumcising themselves, Simeon and Levi, Dinah's brothers, took advantage of the opportunity to massacre them all, killing Shechem and his father in the process (vv.25–6). Jacob reprimanded his sons for carrying out such a reprisal, but they justified their action with a simple question: 'Should our sister be treated like a whore?' (v.31).

The first striking feature of the narrative, from a feminist perspective, is the way in which Dinah herself is marginalized in the account. The entire episode is narrated from a male perspective, and its primary interest is clearly not the violation of Dinah (which occupies a single verse in the entire chapter) but the effect which the incident had upon the male participants in the story. The emotions which Dinah might be expected to have felt (rage, hatred, disgust) are ascribed to her brothers, but their anger is occasioned not so much by the suffering and humiliation endured by their sister as by the shame and disgrace which had befallen their family (v.7). Although it was Dinah who had been raped, it was *their* rights which had been violated, *their* honour which had been impugned and *their* integrity which had been threatened. The concern of the brothers was not with the physical or emotional harm which had been inflicted upon their sister but with the damage that would be caused to their own reputation should she marry an uncircumcised man (cf. Fuchs, 2000, pp.213–14; Fewell and Gunn, 1993, p.84). From the male narrator's viewpoint, the indignity suffered by the family was evidently more important than the abuse suffered by the daughter.

The male perspective of the narrative emerges also from the reaction of Dinah's father, for Jacob's initial response, upon hearing of the incident, was to remain silent (v.5). Far from sympathizing with his daughter's plight and commiserating with her, his immediate concern was that she had been 'defiled' and was, by implication, henceforth unfit to be a bride. Significantly, when Jacob eventually breaks his silence (v.30), it is not to condemn the rape of Dinah but to denounce the excessive violence and cruelty perpetrated by her brothers against the Shechemites.

But the male bias of the account is most clearly evident from the way in which Dinah and her rapist, Shechem, are portrayed. Although it is Shechem who 'takes' (*lāqaḥ*) her, 'lies' (*šākab*) with her and 'rapes' (*'innâ*) her, it is Dinah who is regarded as defiled (vv.5, 13, 27), and in the eyes of her brothers she has been made to appear like a 'whore' (v.31). Indeed, there may even be a hint in the narrative that Dinah was the architect of her own misfortune, for she is depicted as leaving home and 'going out' (*yāṣā'*) of her own volition to visit the women of the region (v.1).[2] While there is no indication that she went with the explicit intention of embarking upon a sexual adventure (cf. Fuchs, 2000, p.207), she would no doubt have been aware that by departing from her home she was leaving behind the security and protection of the family domain.[3]

The portrayal of Shechem the rapist, on the other hand, is by no means as negative as one might have expected.[4] The narrator is careful not to dwell on the rape incident itself (v.2); indeed, the act is reported in such a succinct and restrained manner that attention is deflected from the gravity of the offence. The element of aggression is played down so that the violation of Dinah can almost be viewed as nothing more than a natural extension of male desire. Moreover, by suppressing any hint that she resisted Shechem's sexual advances (contrast the reaction of Tamar, below), the narrator minimizes her suffering, and paves the way for the positive portrayal of Shechem which follows. After the rape incident, Shechem is depicted as speaking affectionately with Dinah and even seeking to make restitution for the wrong which he had committed by expressing his wish to marry her (v.4). By describing his attempt at reconciliation and emphasizing his love for Jacob's daughter (v.3) the narrator shores up sympathy for the rapist; indeed, we almost end up admiring him.

The story of a woman's rape was one which played easily into the hands of the male narrator, for by its very nature it underlined the power of the man and the helplessness of the woman, thus perpetuating the familiar stereotype of the strong, heroic male and the vulnerable, defenceless female. The intervention of Dinah's brothers demonstrates their authority over their female sibling, while at the same time emphasizing her own inability to help herself. Moreover, as soon as the brothers intervene, Dinah quietly disappears from the narrative, and we are not even told what happens to her at the end of the story. The impression given is that Dinah's rape was just an element necessary to trigger off subsequent events; as soon as the incident is over the narrator shifts the focus of the story to the complicated relationship between Jacob and his sons and the power struggle between their tribe and those of the neighbouring communities. Indeed, as Susan Niditch (1992, p.23) has remarked, one of the striking features of the story is the degree to which Dinah is both present and absent in the account. In one sense she is central to the narrative, for she is the focus of Shechem's desire, the object of negotiations between Jacob's sons and Hamor, and the cause of the tension between Jacob and his sons; but on the other hand, Dinah takes no active part in the plot that develops, and she is denied a voice by the narrator. Consequently, the reader is prevented from hearing anything concerning her point of view, and the text offers no clues as to her own thoughts and emotions (Fuchs, 2000, pp.217–19; Aschkenasy, 1986, pp.128–9; Jeansonne, 1990, pp.87–8). We are not told how she reacted to Shechem's advances, or how she responded to the tender words which he subsequently spoke to her. Did she resist her brothers' attempt to release her and express a reluctance to return to a family which considered her to be defiled? Was she pleased that her brothers had killed the only person that she could marry, a man who claimed to love her and who had repented for his violent act? Such questions are not answered because the perspective of the victim was of little interest for the male narrator. His aim was to express male values and male concerns, and the story of Dinah's rape took secondary place to the events which were to unfold after the incident was over.

The narrative recording the rape of Tamar by her half-brother, Amnon, although different in many respects from that concerning the rape of Dinah, provides a further illustration of the male bias of the biblical narrator (2 Sam. 13). Here, in contrast to Gen. 34, there is no attempt to exonerate the rapist of his responsibility for the offence; on the contrary, the detailed description of Amnon's plot to ensnare Tamar by feigning illness (vv.5–6) leaves no doubt as to his culpability, and the premeditated nature of the offence merely serves to make it all the more reprehensible. Even at the beginning of the story the narrator implies that Amnon's intentions were not entirely honourable, for he is said to have been tormented by Tamar's beauty and frustrated because it seemed impossible for him 'to do anything to her' (v.2). Doubts about his intentions increase when he asks David to command her to make some food that he may 'eat from her hand' (v.6). The tension is further intensified when Amnon instructs her to bring the food to his chamber and sends everyone else out of the room (vv.9–10). It thus comes as little surprise to the reader that when Amnon stretches out his hand it is not to seize the food proffered to him but to seize Tamar herself (v.11). When his attempt to persuade her to lie with him fails, he proceeds to rape her.

For her part, Tamar is depicted as doing all within her power to thwart his intentions by appealing to the accepted moral conventions of the nation ('such a thing is not done in Israel'; v.12), to the damage which would inevitably be done to her own self-esteem ('as for me, where could I carry my shame?'; v.13), and to Amnon's own standing in the community ('you would be as one of the scoundrels in Israel'; v.13). Yet, in spite of her unquestioned innocence, and Amnon's palpable guilt, it is Tamar who is made to feel 'shamed'. Moreover, as if to add insult to injury, it is the raped woman, not the rapist, who is punished for the incident. Having been violated and humiliated, Tamar is made to suffer the further ignominy of having her freedom and autonomy restricted by being compelled to remain, 'a desolate woman', in Absalom's house for two years (vv.20, 23). The description of Tamar rending her garment, putting ashes on her head in a gesture of mourning, and going away 'crying aloud as she went' (v.19) underlines her pathetic plight as an abused and rejected rape victim.

As in Gen. 34, there is no explicit condemnation of rape in the narrative, and the violation of Tamar is reported in a cursory fashion ('being stronger than she, he forced her and lay with her'; v.14). By omitting a detailed description of the rape itself, the narrator obviates the need to dwell on the suffering of the victim. Tamar is even made to speak in defence of patriarchal interests by reminding Amnon of his legal obligation to marry her (cf. Ex. 22:16; Deut. 22:28–9), and she is made to appear more outraged by his refusal to do so than she was by the rape itself (v.16). The law which obliged the rapist to marry his victim was presumably designed to relieve the father of the financial burden of having to support a daughter whom nobody else would have wished to marry on account of the loss of her virginity; yet, from the raped woman's point of view, such a law must have appeared offensive and obnoxious in the extreme, for presumably the last thing she would have wanted would have been to marry her assailant. But it is precisely this law, which viewed a woman's rape in terms of the loss of her 'property value' to her father, that Tamar is made to endorse and justify. Despite her ordeal, Tamar emerges from the narrative as one who defends and promotes patriarchal interests; as such, she is the 'perfect rape victim' (Fuchs, 2000, p.216), and her story reflects how, from the male narrator's point of view, a woman ought to react when she had been raped. Moreover, as one who unquestioningly obeys her father's command (vv.7–8) and her brother's wish (v.10), Tamar emerges as the obedient, subservient female responsive to patriarchal domination and control.

Further, although Tamar features more prominently in 2 Sam. 13 than does Dinah in Gen. 34, the story of her rape, too, serves merely as a prelude to the account of male intrigue and conspiracy which follows. The narrator seemingly cares little about the subsequent fate of Tamar; as soon as the rape is over, she virtually disappears from the story and the focus of the narrative shifts to the two brothers. The impression given is that the rape incident was recorded simply in order to explain the reason for the power struggle which subsequently ensued between the male members of her family.[5]

The androcentric focus of the story, however, is most evident in the way in which three of the male characters in the narrative (David, Absalom and Amnon) react to Tamar's rape. In 2 Sam. 13:21, David, her father, is said to be 'very angry' but he does nothing to punish or even rebuke his son, nor does he express any sympathy or compassion for his daughter. Indeed, it is not even clear whether his anger was aroused by the fact that Tamar had been raped or because Amnon, his first-born son, had sunk to such depths of depravity. The reading of the LXX (supported by 4QSam[a]) suggests that David did not punish Amnon because 'he loved him, for he was his firstborn' (cf. *NRSV*); evidently, the affection of the indulgent father for his son was such that he was prepared to overlook even the most serious blemishes in his character. As Trible observes (1984, pp.53–4), David's reaction (or rather his lack of any reaction) leaves little doubt as to where his sympathies really lay.

Absalom's response ostensibly seems more favourably disposed to Tamar, for he is said to have 'hated' Amnon because of the incident and to have refrained from speaking to him (v.22). However, when he meets Tamar after the incident and realizes that she was giving public expression to her despair he asks her to maintain a discreet silence ('be quiet for now, my sister': v.20); evidently, he wanted the matter kept secret, no doubt aware that any attempt to publicize the scandal would impair the authority of the king and tarnish the reputation of the royal household. Moreover, by telling her not to take the matter to heart (v.20), he appears to minimize the gravity of the offence, implying that it was a trivial matter that could easily be ignored. His reaction was not one which was likely to have given much comfort or solace to his abused sister. It is true that Absalom eventually sought revenge for Amnon's outlandish behaviour, but the fact that he expressed no anger at the offence inflicted upon his sister during his initial conversation with Tamar, and that he waited a full two years before retaliating, suggests that his motive was not to revenge Tamar's humiliation (as implied by Jonadab in v.32), but to further his own political ambitions by getting rid of the one who stood between him and the throne (cf. Aschkenasy, 1986, p.140).

But it is Amnon's attitude to Tamar that most clearly reflects the contempt and disdain in which women were held under patriarchy. In contrast to the violation of Dinah, where love blossoms after the rape, Amnon's desire turns to hatred; indeed, he is said to have loathed his half-sister with an intensity which exceeded his earlier passion for her (v.15). Clearly, in Amnon's eyes, Tamar was no more than a sex object which could be cast aside once his sexual appetite had been satisfied. Not content with raping her, he humiliates her further by casting her out in the most degrading and undignified way. Summoning his servant, he instructs him to remove 'this one' (Heb. $z\hat{o}^{\,}t$) from his presence and to bolt the door after her (v.17), giving the impression that it was she who had forced her unwelcome attentions upon him. Thus Tamar, the king's daughter, faces the ignominy of being expelled by a servant, who then locks the door as if she were a repulsive creature against whom every measure must be taken to ensure that she did not return to the house (cf. Bar-Efrat, 1989, pp.268–9).

The stories concerning the rape of Dinah and Tamar illustrate some of the narrative techniques deployed by the male authors to assert patriarchal authority and to shape and perpetuate gender roles and expectations. By denying the victim a voice (Dinah), by portraying the rapist in a positive light (Shechem), by passing over, in the most perfunctory manner, the rape incident itself, by enhancing the part played by the male protagonists while subordinating or marginalizing the role of the female, the biblical narrator guides the reader to view the story from his own perspective. It will now be necessary to examine in more detail some of the strategies used in the narrative tradition of the Hebrew Bible to foster the notion of male dominance and female subordination.

The Marginalization of Women

As was clear from the above narratives, one of the most obvious ways in which the biblical authors sought to foster the ideology of male domination was by marginalizing women and minimizing their role in the events which they recorded. Since patriarchal ideology was based on a belief in the centrality of man it was natural for the biblical narrators to seek to dispatch women to the sidelines and to play down their role as active participants in the story. As Cady Stanton caustically remarked, the biblical writers probably took the same view of women as 'the great Roman General who said "the highest praise for Caesar's wife is that she should never be mentioned at all"' (1895, p.67). In the dramatic stories which captured the imagination of the biblical authors the protagonists are almost invariably male, while the voice of the female is muted, her contribution neglected and her concerns ignored. In large tracts of biblical narratives women are conspicuous only by their absence. They are seldom given the opportunity to speak for themselves and they remain largely invisible in a community counted as adult males. It is true that in a few biblical stories the presence of women dramatically changes the course of events, and that two women (Ruth and Esther) have books named after them, but for the most part they appear mostly as appendages of men and are viewed as secondary characters in the events portrayed. The few token female leaders and prophetesses are merely the exceptions that prove the rule. What we learn from the Hebrew Bible about women is only what the male authors happened to regard as significant, and their activities are often described only in so far as they aid or hinder the plans of the male protagonists. Consequently, the 'history' recorded in the biblical text has become, quite literally, 'his story' (Christ and Plaskow, 1979, pp.63–4), while women are cast in the role of the 'other', the marginal, the insignificant.

The marginalization of women is firmly established in the patriarchal narratives contained in Gen. 12–50, where the females often appear, not as characters in their own right, but as peripheral adjuncts to the lives of the male protagonists. In the stories concerning Abraham and Sarah, for example, the focus is very much on the patriarch, while Sarah is frequently relegated to the margins. It is Abraham who receives the divine call and it is he who is to be blessed and given a son; it is he who will become a great nation and it is his descendants who will be given a land to inhabit (Gen. 12:1–3; 15:18–21; 17:2–8). Sarah, on the other hand, is merely an instrument in the divine plan, a necessary prerequisite if God's promise to Abraham is to be fulfilled. She is excluded from the bond established between God and Abraham and she never comes into 'the privileged locus of her husband's covenantal relationship with Yhwh' (Fuchs, 2000, p.50; cf. Fewell and Gunn, 1993, p.41). Moreover, when Abraham conspires to deceive Pharaoh by passing Sarah off as his sister (Gen. 12:11–13), there is no indication as to whether Sarah was consulted or whether she was a willing or reluctant participant. Significantly, Abraham shows little concern for her welfare; the deception is perpetrated 'so that it may go well with me … and that my life may be spared on your account' (Gen. 12:13). Throughout the incident Sarah is represented as an appendage of her husband, obeying his plan without demur. Of course, her silence served well the ideology of the male author, for had she been allowed to protest against the deception, she might have engaged the reader's sympathy, and emerged as the victim of a callous, exploitative and manipulative husband. Had she expressed outrage or disappointment with Abraham she might have appeared as morally superior to him.[6] It was far preferable to eliminate her words and suppress her point of view; her silence could then be interpreted as complicity with her husband's machinations (Westermann, 1986, p.163). As a character in the Abraham narrative, Sarah thus appears as of only marginal significance. Even when Abraham receives a divine communication to the effect that Sarah's name will be changed and that she will become the ancestress of the people (Gen. 17:15–22) he does not trouble to inform his wife, and she only learns of the promise when she happens to overhear a conversation between her husband and God's messengers (Gen. 18:10).

The sidelining of the female recurs in the subsequent narratives concerning the patriarchs. The promise given to Abraham is passed on through the male line: to Abraham's son, Isaac (Gen. 26:3–5) and then to his son, Jacob (Gen. 28:13–14; 35:11–12). Isaac marries Rebekah, and Jacob marries Leah and Rachel, and, while the matriarchs are not by any means absent from the patriarchal stories, the narrator evinces little interest in their perspective or point of view (cf. Exum, 1993, pp.102–7). Jacob's sons are said to have taken brides from among the daughters of Canaan, but as far as the text is concerned these women are almost completely invisible, presumably hidden from view by the male authors in order to maintain the fiction that this family was composed exclusively of males and that no women – least of all foreign women – formed any part of it. It is true that Jacob's son Judah is said to have married the daughter of Shua (Gen. 38:2), but even her presence was required only by the logic of propagation (Gen. 38:3–5); after all, someone must bear the next generation of sons 'though, as far as the text is concerned, the vast majority of Jacob's sons might have bred, conceived, and delivered children all by themselves!' (Fewell and Gunn, 1993, p.87).

Even when women are brought to the foreground as active participants in the biblical narrative, it is significant that they frequently disappear as soon as they have served their allotted purpose. In the patriarchal narratives women usually appear on the scene only when they are of marriageable age, and the impression given is that, from the story-teller's point of view, they are just a means to an end, that end being the need for biological continuity. Once the male heir is born,[7] and the continuation of the male line ensured, the woman's task is regarded as having been accomplished, and she either recedes imperceptibly into the background or disappears from the narrative altogether. Thus, for example, once Sarah has given birth to Isaac (Gen. 21:1–2) and secured his position as male heir (Gen. 21:8–10) she virtually disappears from the story. As soon as Rachel gives birth to her second son (Gen. 35:16–20), she is no longer necessary for the progression of the narrative; having fulfilled her procreative role, she dies in childbirth and is whisked off the stage (Fuchs, 2000, p.86). After Shua's daughter produces male heirs for her husband, she, too, dies (Gen. 38:12), and as soon as Tamar, Judah's widowed daughter-in-law, manages to ensure the survival of the tribe from which the Davidic monarchy was to emerge, she, likewise, disappears from the narrative (Gen. 38:12–30).

This pattern is by no means limited to the patriarchal narratives recorded in the Book of Genesis. The nameless Shunammite woman who appeals to Elisha to restore her son to life disappears from the story once his survival is guaranteed (2 Kgs 4:18–37). Even Ruth's story comes to an end once she has ensured the continuation of the male line by giving birth to Obed (Ruth 4:13). As Fuchs has observed (2000, p.46), the birth of a son often results in the death of the mother, either literally, as in the case of Rachel, or metaphorically, in the sense that they are 'killed off' in the narrative. As soon as their function *vis-à-vis* the male hero is fulfilled, their usefulness is regarded as having been exhausted, and they disappear from the record. As Ostriker (1993, p.49) has remarked, it is as if 'women must be rejected in order for the story of male maturity, male leadership, male heroism, to take place'.

A further indication of the marginalization of women in the biblical narratives is the fact that they are often not even dignified with a name.[8] Ex. 1:15–2:10 mentions numerous women in connection with the birth and childhood of Moses but, apart from the two midwives, Shiphrah and Puah (Ex. 1:15), they are all nameless.[9] Samson's mother remains anonymous in the biblical account (Judg. 13:1–25),[10] as does Jephthah's daughter who was offered by her father as a sacrifice (Judg. 11:29–40).[11] The 'wise woman' of Tekoa in 2 Sam. 14:1–20 is not named, nor is the medium of Endor whom Saul consulted on account of her professional skills (1 Sam. 28:3–25). The widow of Zarephath, whose son was restored to life by Elijah (1 Kgs 17:8–24) is unnamed in the biblical account, as is the Shunammite woman whose son was similarly restored to life by Elisha (2 Kgs 4:8–37). Solomon is reported to have had seven hundred wives and three hundred concubines (1 Kgs 11:3), but of these only one is named, and then only in passing (1 Kgs 14:21). Even the queen of Sheba remains anonymous, although she figures prominently in the narrative recorded in 1 Kgs 10:1–13. Such women are 'figures' rather than 'characters' in the biblical story;[12] they are denied an identity by the biblical author and effectively assume the status of a non-subject. Of course, there are also many male characters who are anonymous in the biblical accounts, but usually they are obscure, incidental figures who make only a fleeting appearance in the narrative (cf. Judg. 1:24–6; 7:13–14; 8:13–14; 16:26; 1 Sam. 9:5; 2 Sam. 15:15).[13] The striking feature of female anonymity in the Hebrew Bible is the number of women who are unnamed but who are indispensable to the plot of the story in which they appear.[14]

The anonymous status of women in the Hebrew Bible is particularly significant given that in Israel, as in the ancient Near East generally, names carried a special meaning, being the expression of a person's essence and providing an insight into an individual's character or nature (cf. de Vaux, 1965, p.43). Consequently, to deny individuals a name was tantamount to effacing their personal identity. It may well be that the biblical authors had more than one motive for keeping a particular individual anonymous,[15] but it is difficult to avoid the conclusion that, with regard to the female characters, their anonymity was designed to contribute to their marginalization and to the obliteration of their individuality and independence.

Moreover, even when women are named in the biblical sources, they are frequently identified in terms of their male counterparts, being defined as their 'wife', 'daughter' or 'mother' rather than appearing as individuals in their own right. In the narratives discussed at the beginning of this chapter, Dinah is referred to as 'Jacob's daughter' (Gen. 34:7) and as her brothers' sister (Gen. 34:31), and Tamar is referred to by Amnon as 'my brother Absalom's sister' (2 Sam. 13:4). Other examples abound throughout the Hebrew Bible. Sarah, for example, is introduced as 'Abram's wife' (Gen. 12:17) and is referred to repeatedly in the subsequent narrative as 'his wife' or 'your wife' (Gen. 20:2, 7, 11–12, 14). Deborah is introduced as the 'wife of Lappidoth' (Judg. 4:4), and Jael as the 'wife of Heber the Kenite' (Judg. 4:17). Michal is regularly referred to as Saul's daughter and David's wife (1 Sam. 18:20, 27–8; 25:44; 2 Sam. 3:13–14). Bathsheba is introduced as the 'daughter of Eliam' and the 'wife of Uriah the Hittite' (2 Sam. 11:3), a formulation which combines both her father's name and her husband's name. Only very rarely in the Hebrew Bible is a male character introduced as his wife's husband (cf. Ruth 1:3) or as his mother's son (Gen. 36:10–14). By defining women in terms of their affiliation with the men of their lives, the biblical narrators imply that they were of interest only in relation to the male protagonist, and that they were, in effect, merely the possession of their husband or father (Fuchs, 2000, pp.134–5; Exum, 1990, p.45).

The Rebellious Female

Of course, patriarchy was not naïve enough to ignore the role of women completely. Occasionally the male narrator allowed them to figure prominently in the narrative and to occupy a position centre-stage, but in such cases the role which they fulfilled was usually made to serve the interests of patriarchal ideology. Nowhere is this more evident than in the biblical narratives which depict the rebellious female. Such stories recount the fate of women who had the temerity to oppose the patriarchal order, and who refused to conform to the traditional image of the dutiful and subservient female. Instead of acquiescing to male authority and remaining in their allotted domestic sphere, they rebel against the system and set themselves up as the enemies of patriarchy. The stories of Miriam (Num. 12:1–16), Jezebel (1 Kgs 21) and Michal (2 Sam. 6:12–23) provide interesting examples of women who strayed from their approved gender roles and sought to arrogate to themselves a measure of authority equal to that of their male counterparts. At stake in such narratives are issues of authority and power, and the clear implication is that such authority and power are invested in the male. Any attempt by a female to usurp that authority would inevitably lead to humiliation and punishment. The subliminal message of these narratives is clear and uncompromising: women who step out of line and attempt to transcend the usual female destiny will receive their just deserts. Patriarchy 'has God on its side' (Millett, 1969, p.51), and he is a God who will not allow any threat to the gender hierarchy to go unpunished.

Miriam (Num. 12:1–16)

In Num. 12:1–2 Miriam challenges Moses' claim to possess a special relation with God and contends that she is his equal in prophetic authority.[16] Her complaint is rendered in the most emphatic terms, as is clear from the collocation of the two words 'only' (Heb. *raq*) and 'also' (Heb. *'ak*), which occur in such close proximity only here in the Hebrew Bible: 'Has the Lord spoken only through Moses? Has he not spoken through us also?' Moses does not even bother to reply to Miriam's question, and it is left for God to intervene in the sibling rivalry. A divine oracle reaffirms Moses' favoured position, and God proclaims him as his prophet *par excellence* (vv.6–8).

Such a blatant challenge to Moses' authority could not go unpunished, and so Miriam is duly struck with leprosy and excluded from the camp for seven days (vv.10, 15).[17] The fact that Moses had to intercede with God on her behalf (v.13) merely underlined Miriam's subordinate status, and that his intercession proved successful served only to emphasize the extent of his power and influence. From Miriam's point of view, this must have been the ultimate ignominy, for the only way in which she could be cured of her disease was through the mediation of the one whose intimacy with God she had just called into question. As if to add to her humiliation, she is likened by God to a shameful daughter who had so offended her father that he had spat in her face as a sign of his utter contempt (v.14; cf. Bechtel, 1991, p.59). Significantly, after her punishment, Miriam never speaks, nor is she spoken to; she simply disappears from the narrative until the brief announcement of her death and burial in Num. 20:1.

Embedded in this brief narrative is a conflict of gender and, in the power struggle between Moses and Miriam, Miriam loses, and her failure 'embodies the humiliation and defeat of female influence' (Ostriker, 1993, p.44). The narrator clearly had little sympathy for female oppositional voices, and the underlying message of his story is clear: women should stay in their proper place and be satisfied with their lot, and those who had the gall to bid for power and authority would surely pay the price for their defiance and insubordination.

Jezebel (1 Kgs 21)

Various narratives in the Hebrew Bible suggest that Jezebel, by virtue of her character and royal connections, exercised considerable influence in both the religious and the political realm. The precise position which she occupied in the royal palace in Jezreel is unclear. The biblical narrators refrain from alluding to her as 'queen', though this is obviously the position which she occupied in all but name.[18] Her status is evident from the fact that the prophets of Baal and the prophets of Asherah are depicted as eating at her table (1 Kgs 18:19), which implies that she had her own court and sufficient economic means to maintain it (Brenner, 1985, p.22). She was powerful enough to persecute the prophets of Yahweh almost to the point of extinction (1 Kgs 18:4, 13), and her threat to kill Elijah was taken so seriously by the prophet that he was compelled to flee to the south, beyond Israelite territory, in order to escape from her clutches (1 Kgs 19:2–3). The extent of her power is also evident from the fact that Jehu, the founder of the next royal dynasty in Israel, had to murder her before his own rule could be established (2 Kgs 9:30–37). But Jezebel's aggressive and resourceful nature is nowhere more evident than in the familiar story of Naboth's vineyard (1 Kgs 21).

According to this narrative, King Ahab wished to acquire Naboth's property, since it was situated near to his palace in Jezreel, and he is depicted as acting in a perfectly just and reasonable manner in order to obtain it, offering to exchange Naboth's land for a neighbouring vineyard, or else giving him its value in money (v.2). Naboth, however, refused to part with his ancestral inheritance (v.3), and the narrative implies that Ahab accepted his decision, although it evidently caused him some dismay (v.4). From Jezebel's point of view, however, Naboth's refusal constituted an act of blatant insubordination, and she chided Ahab for not exercising his authority as king: 'Do you now govern Israel? ... I will give you the vineyard of Naboth the Jezreelite' (v.7). For Jezebel, the matter was nothing less than a test case of monarchic power and, seeing that her husband was not disposed to act, she took it upon herself to arrange for Naboth to be put to death on a trumped-up charge of blasphemy. She wrote letters in Ahab's name to the dignitaries of Jezreel, requesting them to bring two false witnesses to claim that Naboth had cursed God and king, an offence which would result in his death by stoning (vv.8–10). When she had secured the desired sentence, word was brought to her of Naboth's death (v.14) and she proceeded to inform Ahab that he was now in a position to take possession of the vineyard (v.15). The narrative makes clear that it was Jezebel who single-handedly contrived the judicial murder of Naboth by subverting the due process of law; Ahab, on the other hand, appears as a passive character in the story, and it is implied (vv.15–16) that he was quite unaware of her treacherous act.[19]

Elijah's oracle in vv.20–24, however, indicates that Ahab must accept his share of responsibility for what had happened, and that he must be punished accordingly. The prophet therefore announces that Ahab's male descendants would die prematurely and that his dynasty would come to an end. But it is clear that the narrator regarded Jezebel as the main culprit, and from his point of view no punishment meted out to her could be too cruel or severe.[20] It is difficult not to sense the pleasure that the narrator must have taken in describing the fate which eventually befell her: she was hurled from the lattice window of her palace in Jezreel, and her body was splattered with blood and trampled underfoot by horses; moreover, in accordance with the prophecy of Elijah, her carcass was torn to pieces by dogs, and her corpse turned not to dust but to dung (2 Kgs 9:30–37).

The underlying message of the narrative is clear: such untrammelled power and influence as Jezebel possessed was dangerous and must be curtailed and suppressed. Jezebel was vilified and demonized precisely because she was a woman (and a foreign woman at that) who dared to act independently of the king and who even managed to exercise power over him. As such, she was clearly a threat to the patriarchal system and was to be feared and loathed.

Michal (2 Sam. 6:12–23)

The story of Michal in 2 Sam. 6 provides a further example of a woman who was determined to exercise a measure of autonomy and independence but who was punished for daring to step out of line.[21] The narrative records David's attempt to bring the ark of the covenant to Jerusalem, a move evidently intended to confer religious legitimization upon his rule as king and to confirm his choice of Jerusalem as capital. When the ark was eventually brought into the city after the first attempt proved abortive, it naturally occasioned much joy and celebration, and David was so delighted that he danced before it, clad only in a 'linen ephod' (v.14). When Michal, his wife, saw what was happening through a window, she was so incensed by such an undignified public spectacle that she immediately confronted the king and openly reprimanded him for exposing himself before his subjects. In a rebuke, heavy with sarcasm, she proclaimed: 'How the king of Israel honoured himself today, uncovering himself today before the eyes of his servants' maids, as any vulgar fellow might shamelessly uncover himself' (v.20). Such unseemly behaviour on David's part was regarded by Michal as an affront to the dignity of the office which he held. By his antics, he had shamelessly transgressed the bounds of conventional propriety and had demeaned his royal status.

In the heated quarrel which ensued, however, Michal was put firmly in her place by her contemptuous husband. David angrily rebuked her for having the temerity to criticize the Lord's anointed; as the divinely elected king, he would be the judge of what may and may not be regarded as decorous behaviour. Dismissing his wife's objection, he reminded her that God had chosen him over the fallen house of Saul, her father, and he claimed that he would always be honoured by his humble maidservants even if his behaviour was regarded by his wife as degrading (vv.21–2). At least *they* possessed sufficient religious insight to appreciate that his dance was in honour of the God who had established him upon the throne of Israel.

Although Michal, as depicted by the biblical narrator, was 'hardly a woman to swallow insults in silence' (Alter, 1981, p.125), the marital conflict ended with David having the last word. Michal is denied a right of reply by the narrator, and is silenced for daring to speak out against male authority. Her attempt to assert her independence proved self-defeating, for the quarrel resulted in her permanent estrangement from her husband and in the loss of her status as David's wife (cf. Exum, 1990, pp.51–2). Moreover, she was condemned to die childless (v.23),[22] and as soon as the showdown with her husband was over, she disappears quietly from the narrative.[23]

Again the subliminal message is clear: women who raise a voice of protest against male authority will do so to no avail; indeed, such presumption on their part will only prove to be detrimental to their own interests. No woman who dares to humiliate and disgrace her husband in public will get away with it, and any attempt on her part to act autonomously and assert her independence will inevitably end in dismal failure. Patriarchy has its own way of dealing with such uppity women, and anyone who attempts to destabilize the patriarchal order will find that their punishment will be swift and devastating. Michal provides the classic example of the woman who oversteps the traditional female boundary and who challenges the established role of the wife as docile, subservient and obedient;[24] but she was also a woman who was made to pay the price for refusing to accept her allotted place in society.

Encoded in each of the above narratives is an implicit message about female behaviour. Women such as Miriam, who felt confident enough to bid for the supreme position of community leadership, and who possessed no qualms about challenging male hegemony, would be punished for showing such audacity. Women such as Jezebel, who dared to act independently of their husbands, and who threatened to undermine the patriarchal order, would meet a sorry end. Women such as Michal, who showed contempt and disdain towards their husbands by daring to reprimand them in public, would find themselves estranged from their spouse and forsaken by God.

But just as some narratives suggest that the rebellious female will be punished, others convey the opposite message: women who are dutiful, obedient and submissive will be remembered and rewarded.

The Obedient Female

One of the prime examples in the Hebrew Bible of the obedient female is Jephthah's daughter, whose story is narrated in Judg. 11:29–40. According to this account, Jephthah, prior to a military campaign against the Ammonites, sought a guarantee of success in battle by vowing to Yahweh that, if victory were granted him, he would sacrifice to God the first to emerge from his house upon his return (vv.30–31).[25] The ensuing conflict proved victorious for Jephthah and his army, but his rejoicing was short-lived, for the first to greet him upon his return home was his own daughter, who emerged dancing and playing musical instruments in celebration of her father's success (v.34).[26] Jephthah immediately realized the implication of her untimely appearance, and he bemoaned the fate to which his vow had brought him, rending his clothes as a gesture of utter despair (v.35).[27] His daughter, on the other hand, accepted the inevitable and encouraged her father to carry out his vow, stoically accepting her own role as the sacrificial victim: 'My father, if you have opened your mouth to the LORD, do to me according to what has gone out of your mouth, now that the LORD has given you vengeance against your enemies, the Ammonites' (v.36). She merely asked for a reprieve of two months so that she and her female companions could retreat to the mountains to lament for her unfulfilled life (v.37), a life that must end 'before its potential has unfolded' (Trible, 1984, p.104). Upon her return, the vow was duly implemented, and the death of Jephthah's daughter marked the extinction of his family line.[28] But although she was destined to die without offspring, she was not forgotten, for the women of Israel annually commemorated her death with four days of lamenting during which her tragic story was presumably retold so that it could be remembered from one generation to the next (vv.39–40).

In many respects, the story of Jephthah's daughter provides an effective counterbalance to the narratives discussed above in which the female boldly challenged (Miriam, Michal) or usurped (Jezebel) male authority. Jephthah's daughter made no attempt to oppose the vow which her father had made, nor did she presume to question his judgment or blame him for bringing about her misfortune; on the contrary, she sympathized with his predicament, reminding him that fulfilling the terms of the vow was a just and noble deed, given that Yahweh had secured for him a victory over the enemy. Her words denoted unflinching acceptance and submission, and so she emerges from the narrative as the perfect filial role model, the supreme example of the ideal daughter whose undivided loyalty and obedience to her father knew no bounds (Fuchs, 2000, p.188). Consequently, the memory of her selfless act was allowed to live on and 'she became an example in Israel'[29] of the way daughters should submit to parental authority.

It is not difficult to discern the androcentric propaganda at work in this text. The words which Jephthah's daughter is made to utter to her father ('do to me according to what has gone out of your mouth', v.36; 'let this thing be done for me', v.37) are those which the biblical narrator deemed worthy and admirable for a daughter to say. As Exum has observed, the dialogue is orchestrated in such a way that the daughter is made to speak out against her own interests (1995b, p.76). Her words are used to reaffirm patriarchal authority and to exonerate it of all blame for the entire horrific episode. Moreover, since she made no attempt to protest but accepted her fate with equanimity, she was deemed worthy to be granted an honourable position in Israel's memory and to be elevated to the status of an 'institutionalized heroine' (Fuchs, 2000, p.182). The subliminal message mediated by the text is clear: submit to paternal authority and whatever sacrifice you have to make will be remembered, and even celebrated, for generations to come (Exum, 1993, p.34; 1995b, p.77).

Negative Traits

Another favourite device deployed by the biblical narrators to foster and perpetuate patriarchal ideology was to associate negative traits with women.[30] These often served merely as a foil to bring out the admirable qualities of their male counterparts. Sarah's expulsion of Hagar and Ishmael, for example, contrasts with the compassion and magnanimity shown by Abraham, who generously provided them with food and water for their journey in the wilderness (Gen. 21:8–14). In the subsequent Genesis narratives the women are often depicted as quarrelling, plotting and scheming in order to reach their desired goal, and they display much jealousy and competition over the sexual favours of their shared partners and over their respective procreative abilities (cf. Gen. 30:1). The men, by contrast, act in an altogether more mature way: even as rivals they act with a measure of dignity and decorum, and even when their interests are seemingly irreconcilable they remain gallant and friendly (cf. Gen. 13:8–13; Brenner, 1985, pp.95–6).

The same negative appraisal of the female and positive appraisal of the male recurs in biblical imagery. Negative female images (whore, adulteress, and so on) are regularly applied to the erring people, while positive male images are used of God, who is just and fair. In the marriage metaphor used by the prophets to depict the covenantal relationship between Yahweh and Israel, it is the wife's failure to live up to her obligations that is continually emphasized: she has been unfaithful to her husband (Jer. 3:1–5; 4:30) by going after lovers (Ezek. 16:15–22) and has shown herself to be loose, fickle, stubborn, depraved and untrustworthy (Hos. 2:2–13; Ezek. 23); on the other hand, the husband (God) is depicted as the faithful, long-suffering partner, innocent of all wrongdoing, who has fed, clothed and protected his wife (Hos. 2:8; Ezek. 16:1–14) and who has been prepared not only to reason with her but to forgive her loose, licentious behaviour (Hos. 2:2, 16–20).[31]

Although various negative qualities are associated with women in the Hebrew Bible, two may here briefly be singled out for special mention: their sexuality and their deceptiveness.

Women's Sexuality

In some biblical passages women are viewed as a threat, a temptation and a potential source of discord in society, for they were not averse to using their feminine wiles to exploit the vulnerability of the male and lead him astray. Their sexuality thus came to be viewed in a negative way, and regarded as deviant and potentially dangerous.[32] One such woman who exploited her sexual charms was Delilah (Judg. 16:4–22), whose character encapsulated the negative qualities of seduction, unfaithfulness and treason, and against whom even the powerful Samson was helpless.[33] In Num. 25 the Moabite women in general – and one Moabite woman in particular (Cozbi, v.15) – are portrayed as leading the Israelite men astray from the one true God.

But it is primarily in the Book of Proverbs that women's sexuality is regarded as posing a threat to the stability of the patriarchal order. Women were viewed as the source of disharmony in society, for they were capable of exposing and exploiting the vulnerability of the male and using their charm to lead the unwary astray. Consequently, frequent warnings are given to the young man to avoid the fatal attractions of the loose woman, whose seductive allure and provocative words may well be the cause of his downfall (Prov. 6:23–4; 7:4–5, 10–27). For Israel's sages, the guilt attaching to sexuality is overwhelmingly placed on the female: she is held to be the more culpable party in nearly every sexual liaison, whatever the extenuating circumstances, and any misfortune which might result from an encounter with a loose woman was attributed to her powers of seduction.

Women's Deceptiveness

Deceptiveness is another negative trait which is frequently imputed to women in the Hebrew Bible.[34] Rebekah contrived a plan to deceive Isaac into giving the first-born's blessing to Jacob, her preferred son (Gen. 27:5–29); Rachel stole her father's idols and then feigned ignorance as to their whereabouts when he attempted to find them (Gen. 31:33–5); Tamar dressed up as a prostitute in order to deceive Judah into having sexual relations with her (Gen. 38:12–19); Potiphar's wife tried to deceive her husband into believing that Joseph had seduced her, although he had rejected her advances (Gen. 39:13–18); Rahab deceived her own people in order to assist the Israelite spies (Josh. 2:1–21); Jael deceived Sisera and lulled him into a false sense of security before killing him (Judg. 4:17–22); and Michal deceived Saul for the sake of the persecuted David (1 Sam. 19:11–17).[35] The ploy of depicting women as deceivers served well the interests of patriarchal ideology, for it perpetuated a general mistrust and suspicion of women and implied that they were predisposed to act dishonestly.

Of course, there are also examples of male deceivers in the Hebrew Bible (cf. Otwell, 1977, pp.108–9; Bal, 1988c, p.147; Prouser, 1994, pp.26–7), but, as Esther Fuchs has observed (1985, p.140), the male deceivers often emerge in a favourable light in spite of their deception, for it is implied that they only resorted to such action because they found themselves to be in a particularly dangerous situation. Thus, for example, although Abraham resorted to deception by passing Sarah off as his sister (Gen. 12:10–20), it is emphasized that the circumstances in which he found himself called for such drastic measures, because he felt that his life was in danger (v.12); similarly, Isaac passed Rebekah off as his sister (Gen. 26:6–11) but only because the potential adulterer was the powerful Abimelech, king of Gerar, and the patriarch found himself in a particularly vulnerable position (vv.7, 9). In both cases, the husband is presented as a defenceless victim who attempted to deceive only because he felt that his life was in danger. Even David's deception of Uriah (2 Sam. 11:1–27) is to some extent justified on the ground that Bathsheba had flaunted her naked body at a vantage-point where she could easily be seen by the king (v.2), the implication being that he could not altogether be blamed for succumbing to temptation (cf. Fuchs, 2000, pp.127–8; Fewell and Gunn, 1993, p.157; Exum, 1993, pp.188–9).

Male deceivers are thus exonerated of responsibility for their deception, whereas in the case of female deceivers the biblical narrators often suppress their motivation, thus making it more difficult to view their duplicity in a more favourable light. Significantly, it is only when the deception perpetrated by women serves to promote the cause of men (as, for example, in the case of Jael or Rahab) that their actions are praised and that they are regarded as positive role models (Fuchs, 1985, pp.141–3).

Women as Scapegoats

Another ideological ploy used by the biblical authors was to scapegoat women by assigning to them responsibility for any wrongdoing. One of the most blatant examples of blaming the victim in the Hebrew Bible occurs in the story discussed above (pp.69–70) concerning Jephthah's daughter (Judg. 11:29–40). It is clear from the narrative that it is Jephthah himself who makes the vow to sacrifice to God the first to come out to meet him upon his return from battle (vv.30–31); yet, when he realizes that it is his own daughter who is the first to greet him, he proceeds to blame her for the tragic consequences which would ensue: 'Alas, my daughter! You have brought me very low; you have become the cause of great trouble to me' (v.35a). The emphatic 'you' in the Hebrew serves to emphasize that she is the cause of his calamity and is to blame for the grief which has befallen him. Moreover, by depicting her as coming out of the house of her own accord (v.34), the narrator implies that she was responsible (albeit unwittingly) for her own death. On the other hand, the narrator is careful not to impute any blame to Jephthah himself.[36] He is depicted not as a cruel man who knowingly contrived his daughter's death but as a victim of circumstances beyond his control. Of course, there is a sense in which the fate of both characters is sealed by the tragic event, 'she to die and have no progeny, he to have no progeny and to die' (Exum, 1993, p.20), but the emphasis of the story is that she is ultimately responsible for both her own and her father's demise.

It is primarily in the realm of religious apostasy that women are made to shoulder the blame in the Hebrew Bible. In Deut. 7:1–5 there is concern lest intermarriage with non-Israelite women would make it possible for them to influence their husbands to worship other gods. When the prophets accuse the people of adopting heathen practices it is clear that they regard women as the primary culprits: it is they who wail for Tammuz (Ezek. 8:14) and who prepare offerings for the queen of heaven (Jer. 7:17–18; 44:19).[37] The religious apostasy which was rife in Solomon's day is attributed to his foreign wives who influenced him to follow other deities (1 Kgs 11:1–8). Ahab turned to worship Baal because of the baneful influence of his wife Jezebel (1 Kgs 16:31), who supported the prophets of Baal and Asherah (1 Kgs 18:19). Athaliah, Ahab's daughter, is assigned blame for inducing her husband, Jehoram, and her son, Ahaziah, to do 'what was evil in the sight of the LORD' (2 Kgs 8:16–18, 25–7). Moreover, in the days of Josiah it is women who are singled out as responsible for weaving textiles for Asherah in the Jerusalem temple (2 Kgs 23:7). Deut. 17:17 warned that 'many wives' would 'turn away' a king's heart, and the biblical narrative tradition testifies that women – especially foreign women – did indeed induce the kings of Israel and Judah to follow other deities.

Sometimes the scapegoating of women appears to defy all logic, and nowhere is this more apparent than in the sexual realm. Three cases call for special attention: women are blamed for failure to produce offspring; they are blamed for instigating incestuous relationships; and women are regarded as blameworthy in cases of rape.

Barrenness

In the Hebrew Bible, much emphasis is placed on the importance for the family of having children, especially sons, for this was the means by which one's future welfare and prosperity were secured. Without a male heir, the head of the household could not perpetuate the family line or preserve the ancestral inheritance. Consequently, much joy accompanied the birth of a son, and intense sorrow was felt by a couple who were destined to be childless. The dread of barrenness is heard in Rachel's longing for offspring (Gen. 30:1) and in Hannah's tearful entreaty to God for a son (1 Sam. 1:10–11). It is also evident in the lengths to which women were prepared to go to ensure male offspring, even to the extent of resorting to having children by their handmaid (Gen. 16:2; 30:3).

In the Hebrew Bible, however, it is invariably women who are singled out as the exclusive culprits of childlessness. Thus, for example, the threat to the divine promise of a son for Abraham is occasioned by the fact that it was Sarah who was unable to bear a child (Gen. 11:30); indeed, she herself is made to lament the fact that 'the LORD has prevented me from bearing children' (Gen. 16:2). Isaac is depicted as praying to God for a child because his wife, Rebekah, 'was barren' (Gen. 25:21). Gen. 30:1–8 depicts the suffering that accompanied Rachel's inability to conceive, and 1 Sam. 1:5 describes Hannah, the wife of Elkanah, as childless because God had 'closed her womb'. When a marriage failed to produce children the shame and disgrace invariably fell upon the wife, who was regarded as having failed to fulfil her social obligation and to perform her biological functions. In this regard, Jacob's angry reply to Rachel's plea to be given children is most illuminating: 'Am I in the place of God, who has withheld from you the fruit of the womb?' (Gen. 30:2). The possibility of male impotence or sterility is not even contemplated, for that would have stigmatized the male and derogated from his status, honour and prestige.[38]

Further, as if to add to the barren wife's sense of failure and inadequacy, it is implied that her childlessness was the result of divine retribution for some moral deficiency in her character (cf. Gen. 20:17–18). Just as many children were a sign of divine blessing (Gen. 24:60), so the lack of children was viewed as a sign of divine displeasure (cf. Fuchs, 2000, pp.48–9). Thus women who failed to produce children were not only deprived of the glory and status which attached to motherhood, but were made to bear the burden of guilt for their inability to conceive.

Incest

Gen. 19:30–38 records a case of double incest involving a father, Lot, and his two daughters. The narrative is set in the aftermath of the catastrophe that befell Sodom and Gomorrah, and the daughters, fearing that there were no longer any men available to father their children (v.31), contrived to make their father drunk on two consecutive nights so that they might have sexual relations with him. Both daughters conceived and gave birth to sons, whom they named Moab and Ben-ammi (vv.37–8). Since the sons born of the union subsequently became the tribal ancestors of the later Moabites and Ammonites, the narrative may originally have been intended to slander Israel's traditional enemies (cf. Deut. 23:2–6; Jer. 48:25–6) by associating their origins with dubious sexual liaisons. But the story also served well the interests of patriarchal ideology, for it is the (unnamed) daughters who are depicted as the initiators and perpetrators of the incestuous act. Lot, on the other hand, is emphatically exonerated of all responsibility, for it is made clear that he was quite unaware, in his drunkenness, of what was happening.

By presenting the females as the instigators of the incestuous union, the story reversed the more probable scenario, for daughters were more likely to have been the victims rather than perpetrators of incestuous unions with their father.[39] By holding the daughters responsible the author shifted the blame onto the female characters. Interestingly, the biblical text refrains from any negative judgmental comment on the daughters' act, and their transgression of incest taboos goes unpunished, no doubt because they were deemed to have acted in the interests of patriarchy by seeking to ensure (albeit through the most unorthodox means) the continuation of their father's lineage (v.32).

Another case of incest recorded in the Hebrew Bible involves Judah and his daughter-in-law Tamar.[40] Gen. 38 narrates the marriage of Judah to Shua and records the birth of their three sons Er, Onan and Shelah. Er was married to Tamar but because he was 'wicked in the sight of the LORD' he was slain by God (v.7). Judah then instructed his middle son, Onan, to 'go in to your brother's wife' so that she could have children by him.[41] Onan lay with Tamar but denied her the possibility of becoming pregnant by spilling his semen on the ground (v.9). His action was deemed displeasing to God and he, too, was slain. Dismayed by the course of events, Judah refrained from instructing his youngest son, Shelah, to lie with Tamar, fearing that he might also die prematurely and, in a clear attempt at prevarication, he told her to return to her father's house and wait until Shelah had grown up (v.11). When Tamar realized that Judah had no intention of giving her his youngest son, she devised her own plot to become pregnant. Hearing that Judah (who had by now become a widower, v.12) was due to go to Timnah to visit his sheep-shearers, she took off her widow's clothes and assumed the guise of a prostitute. Judah saw her and expressed a wish to have sexual intercourse with her (vv.15–16) in return for which he promised to give her a kid from his flock. Tamar demanded that he give her a pledge as an assurance that he would send her the kid at a later date, and Judah duly obliged by giving her his signet, cord and staff (v.18). He then had sexual intercourse with her and she conceived by him. Tamar then went away and resumed her role as widow. When Judah learned, some three months later, that his daughter-in-law was pregnant he was so incensed that he instructed that she be burned to death (v.24). Tamar, however, was able to produce the signet, cord and staff as evidence that it was Judah himself who had impregnated her. Faced with such incontrovertible evidence, Judah admitted his guilt and acknowledged his responsibility for unjustly keeping Tamar a childless widow.

This narrative exhibits some striking similarities with the story of Lot and his daughters. In both cases, the male is unaware of the identity of the woman (or women) with whom he is having sexual intercourse, and in both cases it is the female who takes the initiative in instigating the incestuous union. But because the incestuous act is performed in order to ensure the survival of the male line, the females are exonerated of all responsibility for their part in the illicit sexual union. Indeed, Judah was forced to concede that Tamar, by making him face up to his responsibility, was 'more in the right than I' (v.26) even though she had resorted to an act of deception. Thus, although the females in both narratives had instigated a sexual act which was contrary to Israel's law, they are not chastised or condemned, for they had acted in the interests of patriarchal continuity.

Rape

Patriarchal domination often relies on a form of violence, especially of a sexual character, and such violence is nowhere more apparent than in the act of rape. Rape, like incest, is usually viewed as an offence in which the female is the victim, but in the rape narratives recorded in the Hebrew Bible the victims are considered to be the male relatives of the raped woman. For example, in the case of the rape of Dinah, it is not Dinah herself but her father and brothers who are regarded as having been offended by Shechem's outrageous behaviour (see above, pp.55–8). Moreover, as if to add insult to injury, it is the sexually violated woman rather than the rapist who is made to feel ashamed by the incident.[42] Thus in 2 Sam. 13:13 it is not the rapist, Amnon, who feels shame, but his half-sister, Tamar, whom he had raped. Similarly, in Gen. 34:5 it is Dinah, not Shechem, who is regarded as having been 'defiled' by her rape.[43]

Even more reprehensible, from a feminist point of view, is the implication in two of the biblical rape narratives that it was the woman herself who was ultimately responsible for her own misfortune. This may be the point of the observation at the beginning of the Dinah story that she went out by herself to visit the women of the region (Gen. 34:1), the implication being that, had she stayed at home, under the protection of her family, she would not have been raped by Shechem. The same message may be encoded in Judg. 19, which describes the fate of the Levite's concubine, who played the harlot (Heb. *zānā*) against her husband (v.2)[44] and who was subsequently gang-raped by the men of Gibeah (v.25). The implication of the story is that, had she stayed where she belonged, under the authority of her husband, instead of returning to her father's house, she would not have had to endure the horrendous ordeal to which she had been subjected. Such narratives imply in the most subtle way that women may themselves be ultimately responsible for their own violation; if they insisted upon acting in an unconventional manner and (whether deliberately or unwittingly) arousing male sexual appetites, they had only themselves to blame if they became the victims of male sexual aggression (cf. Exum, 1993, pp.188–90).

In Praise of Women

It must not be thought, however, that the attitude of the biblical writers towards women was uniformly negative or hostile. It sometimes served the interests of patriarchy to praise their contribution – provided, of course, that their activity served to promote the interests of their male counterparts. Indeed, it is precisely when women are placed on a pedestal and elevated as paragons of virtue and nobility that the reader needs to be most wary, for even biblical texts that appear to take a positive view of the role of women can have a negative, oppressive impact by stereotyping their role and patronizing their contribution.

The acrostic poem contained in Prov. 31:10–31, which contains a description of the 'ideal wife', provides an interesting case in point. The text praises her ability in managing her household, directing the work of the servants, and providing food and clothing for her family (vv.14–15). But, by extolling the ideal wife as the one whose child-bearing and family-rearing duties are her crowning achievement in life, the text proves to be extremely patronizing and it merely contributes to the familiar stereotyping of women's domestic role. Her contribution is valued in terms of what it provides for her husband and children. She is praised because she contributes to her husband's success in public life and because 'she does him good' (v.12). By directing her talents and energy to the mundane household chores, her husband is relieved of domestic worries and is able to sit 'among the elders of the land' (v.23) and exert influence upon the life of the community (cf. Fuchs, 2000, p.174, n.64; Bird, 1974, pp.55–6). It is little wonder that she is regarded as 'far more precious than jewels' (v.10) and that she earns the praise of her husband (v.28), for everything which she does is directed at enhancing his reputation and ensuring his family's well-being.

Given that the ideal wife in Prov. 31:10–31 is praised on account of her care and concern for her family, it is hardly surprising that it is primarily mothers who are singled out for admiration and approval in the Hebrew Bible. Motherhood was regarded as a role of honour and, as we have seen, child-bearing was viewed as a sign of divine blessing. Here the male-centred ideology of the biblical authors is clearly visible, for mothers are praised because they have channelled their energies to achieve a patriarchal goal, namely, the perpetuation of the male line. After all, it was primarily in the interests of the husband that sons were produced: they served to enhance *his* prestige and would eventually contribute to the prosperity and productivity of *his* household. But, while the patriarchal ideology is here unmistakable, it is also very subtle, for the interest of the father in producing male progeny is played down and the impression given is that it was the mother who was primarily concerned to ensure the perpetuation of the male line (cf. Fuchs, 2000, p.48).

Thus, for example, it is Tamar who is depicted as going to excessive lengths to ensure that Judah has male progeny, and it is Ruth who will stop at nothing to ensure the genealogical continuity of her husband's deceased family. Both women, in fact, deploy questionable means to secure their goal, exploiting their sexuality in order to compromise the gullible male whom they wished to attract. Yet, although their dubious acts clearly invited negative moral evaluations, the biblical authors desist from condemning them; on the contrary, they are admired for their resourcefulness and determination and regarded with approval, for their actions were seen to 'advance the well-being of patriarchy' (Bos, 1988, p.38; cf. Brenner, 1985, pp.107–8). Of course, the irony is that both women, despite having risked their reputations, would be omitted from the patriarchal genealogy which they were evidently so anxious to sustain.

Conclusion

The above discussion has shown that in the transmission of the biblical traditions, narratives concerning women received a strongly patriarchal slant. We have sought to examine the literary strategies by which the biblical authors excluded and marginalized women, and have attempted to reveal the subtle (and sometimes not so subtle) methods deployed by them to maintain patriarchal power and control. Sometimes they merely played down the role of women in the unfolding of events, ensuring that, once they had served their allotted narrative purpose, they disappeared from the story. At other times, the biblical authors deliberately attributed negative characteristics to women, shifting the blame for the foibles of society firmly onto their shoulders. The biblical authors occasionally praised women's contribution, but usually on condition that it served to further patriarchal ends.

By examining various elements in the narratives (dialogue, plot, characterization) our aim has been to draw attention to the patriarchal value systems which they presuppose, and to indicate some of the ways in which the narrator guides the reader to accept his own version of events. Of course, it was important for the narrators that they carry the reader along with them, for their purpose was not just to describe a male-dominated society but to defend and justify it. Within the biblical narratives there is clearly 'a rhetoric of persuasion' at work (Fuchs, 2000, p.15). How feminist critics should deal with such a 'rhetoric of persuasion' will be examined in the next chapter.

Notes

1   Some have argued that Gen. 34:1–4 is not concerned with rape, as such, since the Hebrew verb ʿ*innâ* means 'to humiliate' and carried no suggestion that force was used (see Bechtel, 1994, pp.19–36; 2000, p.70; cf. also Frymer-Kensky, 1989, p.100, n.9; 1998, p.87). But, as Westermann (1986, p.538) observes, the verb here, as in other contexts (cf. Judg. 20:5; 2 Sam. 13:12) conveys the sense of 'forceful violation'. Moreover, Shechem's offer to marry Dinah (v. 4) suggests that he was acting in accord with the demand of the law that rapists should be made to marry their victims (Ex. 22:16; Deut. 22:28–9).

2   Cf. Brenner (1997b, p.170). It is worth noting that the verb *yāṣāʾ* ('go out') is replete with sexual connotations in Hebrew.

3   Cf. Frymer-Kensky (1998, pp.86–7). Some of the rabbis understood the text to imply that Dinah, by behaving in such an unconventional manner, got what she deserved and

brought about her own downfall (cf. *Midrash Rabbah* 80:2). See Aschkenasy (1986, pp.129–30), Graetz (1993, pp.312–13).

4   Fewell and Gunn argue that the narrator in Gen. 34 was intent upon tipping the balance in favour of Shechem (1991, p.197); for a different view, see Sternberg (1992, pp.463–88).

5   Cf. Aschkenasy (1986, p.138). This is implied in the headings given to 2 Sam. 13 in some modern translations. *NEB* has 'Absalom's Rebellion and other Conflicts', while *REB* has 'Conflict in David's Family'. The implication is that Tamar's rape is 'of limited interest in itself, only an historical basis for the real political issues of the remaining chapters of Samuel' (Hammond, 1992, pp.63–4).

6   Fuchs suggests that the morally inferior wife is 'one of the fundamental principles of patriarchal ideology' (2000, p.143).

7   As many feminist biblical critics have observed, there are hardly any accounts of the birth of daughters in Genesis. It is true that Gen. 30:21 records the birth of Dinah, the last child born to Leah, but even her birth is eclipsed by the arrival of Rachel's first-born son, Joseph (Gen. 30:22–4). See Rashkow (1994, pp.22–3).

8   For the view that the namelessness of women is 'one of the strategies to achieve their oblivion', see Bal (1988a, p.6). According to Meyers, the Hebrew Bible contains a total of 1426 names, of which only 111 are the names of women, a statistic which she regards as a glaring demonstration of the 'male-centred concerns of biblical literature' (1992, p.245). Bohmbach similarly regards it as 'a stunning reflection of the androcentric character of the Bible' (2000, p.34). In the volume edited by Carol Meyers (2000), which provides a comprehensive listing of all the women in the Bible, the section on named women comprises 129 pages, whilst that on unnamed women comprises 328 pages.

9   Moses' mother, who appears in this account, is later identified as Jochebed (Ex. 6:20) and his sister is later identified as Miriam (Num. 26:59). Later tradition bestowed many names on Pharaoh's daughter (Thermutis, Meris, Batya, Sephura, Damaris); cf. Tal Ilan (1993, pp.42–4).

10   Later Jewish commentators, however, did provide her with a name. In Pseudo-Philo she is called Eluma (*BibAnt.*, 42) and in *b. Baba Batra* 91*a* her name is given as Zlelponith, while in *Numbers Rabbah* 10:5 she is named Hazlelponi (cf. Reinhartz, 1998, p.183). For a discussion of post-biblical names of biblical women, see Tal Ilan (1993, pp.3–67).

11   As Fuchs has observed, the anonymity of Jephthah's daughter is particularly ironic given the impression created in the narrative that she would never be forgotten in Israel (2000, p.193). Schüssler Fiorenza (1983, p.xiii) cites a parallel example in the New Testament in the case of the nameless woman who anointed Jesus and of whom Jesus said 'what she has done will be told in remembrance of her' (Mk 14:9).

12   Barthes (1974, pp.67–8) argues that in order to have a 'character' there must be a proper name; without such an appellation the individuals concerned remain merely 'figures'. Cf. also Bal (1987, pp.106–7).

13   Such figures are referred to by Reinhartz as 'bit players' and usually function in the role of servants, stewards, armour-bearers or messengers (1998, pp.19–44).

14   The anonymity of Samson's mother, for example, is particularly striking, given the central role which she plays in Judg. 13. See Exum (1980, p.48), Reinhartz (1992, pp.25–37).

15   One reason for the introduction of anonymous figures into the narrative may have been to draw attention to the more significant named characters with whom they interact; another may have been to draw attention away from the character's personal identity to his or her typified role. See Reinhartz (1998, p.96).

16   In the present form of the text, the challenge to Moses' authority is attributed to both Aaron and Miriam, but since the verb 'spoke' in Num. 12:1 is in the feminine singular, the reference to Aaron is commonly regarded as a later addition. Moreover, that Miriam alone was the one who instigated the complaint seems to be confirmed by the subsequent narrative, for only she is punished for showing such insubordination. Cf. Davies (1995, pp.113–26), Burns (1987, pp.68, 72).

17   The rabbis accepted the justice of the punishment of leprosy, and regarded Miriam as a warning to all slanderers (cf. *Num.R.* 16.6–7). Apart from this incident, Miriam is generally praised by the rabbis; indeed, were it not for the defiance which she exhibited in Num. 12, she would be 'one of the few women in the Bible about whom the rabbis have nothing bad to say' (Graetz, 1994, p.235).

18   Brenner (1985, p.20) suggests that Jezebel's position was that of a co-regent.

19   It may be, however, that in the original form of the story the real culprit was Ahab, for the inclusion of Jezebel in the judgment oracle of Elijah in v.23 is commonly regarded as a secondary addition. Rofé (1988, pp.89–104) suggests that Jezebel's treachery was introduced into the narrative by a later post-exilic editor, whose shifting of the blame to a foreign woman formed part of that era's polemic on the dangers of inter-marriage. Miller (1967, pp.313–17) goes so far as to suggest that the tradition in its original form concerned not Ahab but Jehoram, since the fulfilment of Elijah's prophecy occurs in the narrative of Jehu's *coup d'état* recorded in 2 Kgs 9.

20   As Fewell and Gunn have observed, it is difficult to find an example of deeper hostility anywhere in Kings than that heaped upon Jezebel (1993, p.165).

21   On the biblical portrait of Michal, see the anthology of writings edited by Clines and Eskenazi (1991).

22   Some scholars interpret her childlessness as an indication of Michal's refusal to have further sexual relations with David on account of his outrageous behaviour (cf. Clines, 1991, p.139); others argue that it was David who ceased to have further conjugal relations with her after her emotional outburst (Porter, 1954, pp.165–6). It is probable, however, that the biblical author intended her childlessness to be seen as 'a divine judgment of the supercilious wife who dared taunt the divinely chosen king' (Fuchs, 2000, p.142).

23   As Exum observes (1992, p.81) Michal is 'denied children and voice (and thereby narrative presence) in one fatal stroke'. Michal does make one further appearance in 2 Sam. 21:8–9, where it is stated that David handed over her five sons to the Gibeonites to be executed. However, in view of the reference in 2 Sam. 6:23 to Michal's childlessness, many versions (cf. *REB, NRSV, NIV*) prefer to read Merab instead of Michal in 2 Sam. 21:8–9 (following a number of ancient manuscripts), Merab being the name of Michal's older sister (cf. 1 Sam. 18:19).

24   Berlin (1982, pp.71–2; 1994, pp.24–5) argues that, throughout 1 Sam. 18–20, Michal emerges as a decidedly 'unfeminine' character, in contrast to Jonathan, who was perceived by the narrator as possessing feminine traits.

25   Commentators are divided as to whether Jephthah had in mind a human or animal sacrifice (cf. Marcus, 1986, pp.13–18). The language of v.31*b* would normally refer to the latter, but the description in v.31*a* seems to envisage someone welcoming the victor upon his return from battle. In any event, Jephthah's response in v.35 makes clear that he certainly did not expect to be greeted by his only child.

26   The actions attributed to Jephthah's daughter in v.34 are redolent of other biblical scenes in which women celebrate a military victory by coming out to meet the returning conquerors with music and dancing (1 Sam. 18:6–7; cf. Ex. 15:19–21).

27   The tragic dimension of the narrative is made all the more poignant by the fact that Jephthah is depicted as having been empowered with God's spirit prior to the battle (Judg. 11:29) and would thus presumably have been assured of success even if the vow had not been uttered. The vow which he made was therefore redundant and unnecessary, and the dire consequences which resulted from it could have been avoided. Cf. O'Connell (1996, p.183), Exum (1992, p.49).

28   This is clearly what is implied by the information that Jephthah's daughter was his only child (a point made most emphatically in v.34*b*) and that she was a virgin (v.37). No mention is made in the narrative of Jephthah's wife; thus the possibility of further offspring seems to be precluded.

29   For this rendering of the problematic phrase *wattᵉhî-ḥôq bᵉyiśrā'ēl*, see Exum (1992, p.66); cf. Trible (1984, pp.106–7).

30 The effects of negative and stereotypical representations of female characters has been an important focus of debate within secular feminist theory; cf. Mills (1994, p.30).

31 Shields (1995, pp.61–74) notes that in Jer. 3:1–4:4 the metaphor of the promiscuous wife is used to depict the sinful nation, but when reconciliation is envisaged there is a subtle shift in the prophetic imagery, and the people are addressed as 'sons'.

32 Millett (1969, pp.51–4) argues that one of the most effective agents of patriarchal control was its attribution to the female of the dangers and evils it imputes to sexuality.

33 Bal (1987, p.38) regards the story of Samson and Delilah as the 'paradigmatic case of woman's wickedness' in the Hebrew Bible.

34 Deceptiveness is regarded by Fuchs as 'an almost inescapable feature of femininity' in the Hebrew Bible (1985, p.137), and she argues that the tactic of associating deception with women in particular has been 'among the most successful strategies of traditional patriarchies' (1988, p.69). On women as deceivers in the Hebrew Bible, see Prouser (1994, pp.15–28).

35 Feminist critics argue that the biblical examples of female deception are a sign of the socially disadvantaged position of women in a patriarchal society, for only by resorting to such methods could they hope to influence the course of events (Steinberg, 1988, pp.6–7; Fuchs, 1985, pp.137–9).

36 The rabbis, on the other hand, did place the responsibility for the sacrifice of Jephthah's daughter firmly upon his shoulders, no doubt in an attempt to absolve God of any responsibility in the matter. See Valler (1999, pp.48–66).

37 Bird (1997, p.100) suggests that the prophetic use of the metaphor of the promiscuous bride to describe Israel's apostasy may reflect a special proclivity on the part of Israelite women for foreign cults.

38 Lest any doubts be raised concerning the fertility of the patriarchs, it is emphasized that both Abraham and Jacob already had sons when their sterile wives, Sarah and Rachel, finally conceived. Cf. Exum (1993, pp.120–21).

39 Cf. Fuchs (2000, p.177), Fewell and Gunn (1993, p.64), Brenner (1997b, p.101). This is, in fact, recognized in the legal texts, for it is the male addressees who are the subject of the incest laws (Brenner, 1994a, p.115). It is striking, however, that in the list of twelve categories of forbidden sexual relations with females recorded in Lev. 18:7–18, and in the seven categories listed in Lev. 20:11–21, there is no prohibition of father–daughter incest. Cf. Brenner (1994a, pp.120–22), Rashkow (1994, pp.27–8).

40 That the biblical notion of incest extended beyond blood relationships to include in-laws is clear from Lev. 18:15; see Brenner (1997b, p.91).

41 Deut. 25:5–10 required the brother of a deceased man who had died without progeny to marry the widow; the children born of such a union would have been regarded as the dead man's children. On the law of the levirate marriage, see Davies (1981b, pp.138–44, 257–68).

42 Cf. Fewell and Gunn (1997, p.26). Schüssler Fiorenza (1998, p.151) argues that the contemporary cultural pattern of making the victim of rape feel guilty and ashamed is due in no small measure to the pernicious impact of the teaching of the Bible. See also Thistlethwaite (1985, pp.96–107), Fewell and Gunn (1993, p.32).

43 As Fuchs has remarked, rape in the Hebrew Bible is a crime that 'stigmatizes the victim, not the victimizer' (2000, p.215).

44 To 'play the harlot' or to 'commit fornication' is the usual meaning of the Hebrew verb *zānā*, though many modern translations prefer here to follow the rendering of the LXX and read 'she became angry with him' (cf. *NRSV*).

Chapter 5

Ideological Critique

In the previous chapter we sought to expose the gender ideology of the biblical text and to outline some of the strategies deployed by the biblical authors to promote and foster their own patriarchal agendas. Such an exercise was deemed necessary, for only when the patriarchal bias of the text has been identified can it properly be discussed and critiqued. Once readers are made aware of the literary devices used in the Hebrew Bible to perpetuate male domination, they are better placed to resist the ideology of the text and to develop counter-strategies of their own.

For example, we have seen that one of the literary devices deployed by the male biblical narrator was to marginalize women and play down their influence in the unfolding of events. Many feminist biblical critics have therefore developed a counter-strategy either by highlighting the role of women in the biblical text or by making their presence more visible in the events of biblical history. They envisage their task as being to rescue the women of the Bible from their shadowy existence (Bos, 1988, pp.37–67) and believe that only by confronting the extent of their exclusion from Scripture can their real contribution be properly appreciated.[1] Of course, the task of feminist biblical scholars is inevitably hampered by what they regard as the conspiracy of silence which surrounds the male-authored texts. Since the biblical authors have deliberately suppressed the contribution of women from the biblical record the only option for feminist critics is to attend to the hidden and marginal aspects of Scripture and to pay attention to the 'unsaid' (Camp, 1997, p.86).

Some feminist biblical critics have broached this task from an historical perspective and have sought to ensure that the contribution of women in biblical history has not been skewed or distorted by the male authors; others have been concerned more with the literary representation of women, and have sought to highlight the process of textual editing by which the role of women of influence and power has been obscured, forgotten or erased. But while such attempts have proved popular and have yielded potentially valuable results, the methodologies deployed in each case have their limitations.

A Hermeneutic of Historical Reconstruction

This hermeneutical approach involves reaching beyond the androcentric biblical texts to recover – often with the aid of insights drawn from the realm of sociology, anthropology or archaeology – the social reality which the biblical authors have contrived to keep hidden. Carol Meyers, for example, has used social–anthropological and archaeological evidence in an attempt to reconstruct the ordinary lives of women obliterated by the patriarchal text, and she claims to be able to provide a far more positive assessment of their role and influence in ancient Israel than that which is suggested by the biblical tradition (1988, pp.139–64; cf. Hackett, 1985, pp.15–38; 1992, pp.87–8). She argues that, in the decentralized village life of the pre-monarchic period, women enjoyed a relatively high status in society and were integrally involved in the economic, political and cultural affairs of the community. Owing to the virtual absence of public functionaries the household assumed a prominent role in controlling key aspects of social life. Within the household, the woman held a pivotal place, and in such a society female power was 'as significant as male power, and perhaps even greater' (Meyers, 1988, p.176).

In a similar vein, Schüssler Fiorenza has attempted an historical–critical reconstruction of the position of women in the early Christian community and, by highlighting the contributions of those whom the text has marginalized, she claims to have discovered a positive aspect to women's role in history that has been neglected, ignored or forgotten by the male-dominated biblical authors. The paucity of information in the biblical sources concerning the contribution of women should not be regarded as a sign of their inactivity or their unimportance; rather, it was due to the androcentric bias of the biblical traditions and the patriarchal nature of the culture from which they emerged (1979, pp.84–92; 1983, pp.41–56). The biblical writers, influenced by the values and assumptions of that culture, deliberately minimized the role of women and transmitted only a fraction of the traditions concerning their contributions to the early Christian movement. This was why it was necessary for feminist scholars who attempted to reconstruct early Christian history to look behind and beyond the writings of the biblical canon, for only thus could they 'reclaim this history as the history of women and men' (1983, p.xiv). The few biblical passages in which women play a crucial role are regarded as 'the visible tip of an iceberg which for the most part is submerged' (Schüssler Fiorenza, 1985, p.134). Such passages, together with various random details mentioned in passing, are viewed as indicators that women figured prominently in the religious life of the early Christian communities, and that their influence within those communities was more significant and far-reaching than has hitherto been recognized.

It is clear that Meyers and Schüssler Fiorenza have a common goal, namely, to reclaim women's contribution to Israel's history and to the history of the Early Church. By drawing attention to neglected traditions, and reinterpreting familiar ones, they believe that they can reconstruct a scenario in which women were at the centre, rather than at the periphery, of events, and by retrieving from the text that which the authors were trying to silence they claim that the reality of women's experiences can be recovered and restored as part of the normative tradition.

Now it is perfectly natural that a feminist critique of Scripture should want to seize upon the affirmative dimensions of women's role in Israel's history and to ensure that their contribution should not remain unnoticed and unappreciated. But, while the aim of feminist biblical critics such as Meyers and Schüssler Fiorenza seems perfectly commendable, the methodology deployed by them is open to question. The fact is that much of the information needed for this type of historical reconstruction is, for the most part, unavailable and unrecoverable (from biblical or extra-biblical sources), and consequently the results achieved must be regarded as highly speculative, based, as they often are, upon arguments from silence. For these scholars, what is omitted from the biblical text is just as significant as what is documented, and what is absent is just as telling as what is present (Schüssler Fiorenza, 1999, pp.80–81). But the problem with such an assessment of the biblical evidence is that the role which is attributed to women in the history of Israel and in the early Christian movement is often made to appear more significant and influential than the biblical sources will allow. Indeed, Schüssler Fiorenza readily concedes that the lack of solid evidence invites the feminist biblical critic to indulge in a process of 'imaginative reconstruction', and she argues that it is perfectly legitimate to fill in the gaps in the narratives in order *'to create* [my italics] narrative amplifications of the feminist remnants that have survived in biblical texts' (1985, p.135).

It may well be that such gaps in the texts have a *literary* significance (see below) but whether they can be deemed to have an *historical* significance is quite another matter. The impression given is that practitioners of this approach indulge in a kind of wishful thinking as they try to reconstruct what the text does not explicitly say, and one is inevitably left wondering whether the resulting picture of the role and influence of women in the community of faith is real or idealized.[2] Of course, Meyers may well be correct in stating that the biblical text is not coterminus with Israel's history and that social reality 'did not necessarily coincide with what appears in the official canonical documents' (1988, p.41), but it does not follow that the patriarchal nature of Israelite society was a creation of the biblical authors or that the 'Jesus movement' was originally an egalitarian enterprise (Schüssler Fiorenza, 1993a). It may well be that in this regard the male-dominated texts are an accurate reflection of historical reality and that there never was a time when women had a particularly significant or authoritative role either in the social world of ancient Israel or in the development of the early Christian community (cf. Loades, 1998, p.90).

This is not to say that valuable insights have not been gained by the application of such 'historical' approaches to the biblical text; indeed, many interesting readings of familiar passages have emerged as a result of such studies. But attempts to reach 'behind the text' to recover knowledge about the actual conditions of women's lives in the biblical period are fraught with problems, and the conclusions reached must be regarded as highly tentative and hypothetical.

A Hermeneutic of Literary Reconstruction

Other feminist biblical critics have sought to highlight the role of women, not in Israel's history, but in the literary creations encountered in the Hebrew Bible. They conceive their task as being to rewrite women back into the text and to break the conspiratorial silence regarding their role in the biblical narrative. Just as literary devices were deployed by the biblical authors to marginalize women, so can literary strategies be developed by feminist scholars to recover their role and significance in the narrative tradition.

For example, there are some indications in the Hebrew Bible to suggest that Miriam occupied a position of prominence and prestige in Israel. In Ex. 15:20 she is called a 'prophet', and Mic. 6:4 names her, along with Moses and Aaron, as leaders of the people during the exodus and wilderness wanderings. In Ex. 15:20–21 she is depicted as leading the women in a victory dance by the Red Sea, and Num. 12:2 suggests that she was bold enough to challenge Moses' authority. But while the biblical text gives tantalizing hints of Miriam's importance and influence, she is not accorded the attention the few passages concerning her suggest she deserves. Indeed, the very texts that hint at Miriam's significance at the same time manage to undercut it (cf. Plaskow, 1990, pp.38–9). Thus, for example, although she is depicted as a leader, there is no account in the Hebrew Bible of her rise to a position of leadership, and although she is called a 'prophet', there are no examples of her prophecies or any clues as to the nature of her prophetic activity. Why the male narrators should have conspired to play down her role and significance can only be surmised. Perhaps she was perceived to be a threat to the patriarchal order (cf. Num. 12:2) or perhaps it was thought that any attention lavished upon her might detract from Moses' role as the real leader and hero of the people. But, whatever the reason, Miriam's role was minimized and suppressed by the biblical authors and her contribution was practically submerged within the male-oriented framework of the biblical text.

This process of redactional bias is perhaps most clearly exemplified in the so-called 'song of Miriam' preserved in Ex. 15:21. The impression given in the biblical text is that the one stanza which she sang at the sea was merely an abridgment of the much lengthier song attributed to Moses in Ex. 15:1–18. The redactors manage to imply that Miriam's contribution was secondary and derivative, whereas Moses' contribution was primary and original; he could sing an entire poem, whereas she could cite only a single stanza (cf. Trible, 1989, pp.14–25). Literary–critical studies, however, suggest that the original song of Miriam was the version contained in Ex. 15:1–18,[3] and some have surmised that it may have belonged to a corpus of women's compositions which included the Song of Deborah (Judg. 5:1–31) and the Song of Hannah (1 Sam. 2:1–10; cf. Trible, 2000, p.128). Although the biblical editors attributed the song to Moses, no doubt in an attempt to elevate his status, the tradition associating it with Miriam proved so tenacious that it could not be eradicated completely, and so it was appended in a truncated form to the longer Moses version. The case of Miriam provides a particularly good example of the way in which traditions that were suppressed by the biblical authors or redactors are recovered and restored by feminist biblical scholars.

Occasionally, however, the task faced by feminist biblical critics is not to recover lost traditions so much as to highlight traditions which are already present in the biblical text. By reading the biblical narratives carefully and taking into account their overarching perspective, female characters are seen to play a more significant role than is frequently realized, and their contribution to the development of the story is more crucial than is often appreciated. For example, although Abraham is ostensibly the protagonist in the narratives recorded in Gen. 12–25, it is arguable that it is Sarah who is instrumental in moving God's promise to its ultimate fulfilment (cf. Jeansonne, 1990, pp.14–30). It is she who suggests a solution to the problem caused by her childlessness by offering to give her Egyptian maid, Hagar, to her husband so that he could obtain an heir through her (Gen. 16:2–3). Moreover, when Sarah's status as the primary wife appears to be in jeopardy, it is she who acts decisively to safeguard her own position (Gen. 16:4–6). Later, it is she who protects Isaac's inheritance by having Hagar and Ishmael sent away (Gen. 21:10), and although Abraham balks at the thought of expelling them from his household, Sarah's action is said to have won divine approval (Gen. 21:12). Thus, although Abraham might *appear* as the major character in the story, a closer examination of the narrative reveals that Sarah's role and influence was more far-reaching than might appear on a superficial reading of the story (Exum, 1985, pp.75–8).

The narrative concerning Rebekah provides a similar case in point (Exum, 1985, p.78). Although Gen. 25–36 appears to be concerned primarily with Jacob, it is Rebekah who often plays the central role in the unfolding of events. It is she alone who receives a divine revelation that her sons will give rise to two nations, information to which her husband, Isaac, is not privy (Gen. 25:22–3). Moreover, it is Rebekah who is instrumental in determining which son will be the next recipient of the patriarchal promise and blessing. It is she who conceives the plan to dress Jacob up in Esau's clothes so that he will be able to deceive his blind father (Gen. 27:1–17) and, after the deception proves successful, it is Rebekah who again takes control of events by engineering Jacob's safe passage away from the vengeance of Esau who was intent upon killing him (Gen. 27:41–28:5).

Feminist biblical critics thus argue that it would be grossly misleading to view characters such as Sarah or Rebekah as minor players in the unfolding drama; on the contrary, they exercise considerable power and influence in their own right within the context of the narratives in which they appear. They are depicted as taking crucial decisions and it is they who are largely responsible for ensuring that the divine plan reaches its fulfilment.

Of course, feminist biblical critics concede that there are some cases in the Hebrew Bible where women are clearly cast in a subsidiary role, but they argue that even here their contribution is often critical for the way in which subsequent events unfold. Ex. 1:15–2:10, for example, shows how the redemption of the Hebrews from the land of Egypt was made possible by the fortitude, courage and determination of a group of (mostly unnamed) women who resolutely refused to bow to male authority (Trible, 1989, pp.14–25; Siebert-Hommes, 1994, pp.62–74). The story records how two midwives were prepared to defy Pharaoh's command to kill the male Hebrew infants (Ex. 1:15–21); how the resourcefulness shown by Moses' sister at a crucial moment determined his fate (Ex. 2:4–8); and how Moses' mother and Pharaoh's daughter openly disobeyed Pharaoh's command (Ex. 2:8–10; cf. 1:22). As Exum remarked, 'without Moses there would be no exodus, but without these women there would be no Moses!' (1985, p.81; cf. 1994, p.52).

While the strategy of recovering and highlighting women's role in the biblical narrative tradition provides a much-needed corrective to the predominant emphasis on the part played by the male protagonists, the weakness of the approach is its failure to take account of the ideology of the biblical authors.[4] However significant the part played by women in the events recorded, the fact is that they usually function to further patriarchal interests. Thus, for example, although Sarah and Rebekah play a decisive role in determining the future of Israel, it is their sons who feature prominently in the subsequent tradition. While the matriarchs act with courage and fortitude, their actions are motivated by a maternal concern to prosper and further the careers of their male offspring. Their power is not the power of people who are in a position of authority; rather, theirs is a vicarious power that achieves success for themselves through the accomplishments of their male offspring (Niditch, 1992, p.20). Likewise, despite the significant part played by women in Ex. 1:15–2:10, their activity centres on the male infant, Moses, and it is left for *him* to effect the actual liberation of the Hebrews and to become the leader of the people. Indeed, once Moses' survival is ensured, most of the female participants disappear from the story and are heard of no more. Thus, to emphasize the prominence of women in the biblical narratives is merely to play into the hands of the male narrators, for, from a feminist perspective, there is little point in highlighting the role of women in the biblical narrative if all they do is act 'behind the scenes' to promote patriarchal interests.

Any discussion of the role of women in the biblical narrative tradition must therefore take seriously the ideology of the text. If women are marginalized by the biblical narrator and consigned to a peripheral role in the story, the feminist critic must consider whether this is part of a deliberate strategy to undermine their role and influence. The 'gaps' in the text are therefore significant, not because of what they tell us about the actual role of women in the history of Israel or in the development of the Early Church, but because of what they tell us about the aim, purpose and ideology of the biblical author. The omissions and silences in the text are part of a narrative technique deployed by the male narrators in order to promote and perpetuate their patriarchal interests. What is needed, therefore, is a critique of the ideology latent in the biblical texts, and one of the most effective ways of accomplishing this task is to apply what feminist critics have termed a 'hermeneutic of suspicion' to their content.

A Hermeneutic of Suspicion

This hermeneutical approach demands that readers be suspicious of the text's ideological innocence and that they learn to question its underlying assumptions. Instead of reading biblical passages at face value they must ask some searching questions of the text. For example, what androcentric agenda does the author of a particular narrative try to promote? Why does he portray women in the way he does? Do the female characters in the story speak and act only to promote the interests of their male counterparts? Are they being used by the male narrator to support the patriarchal system? In brief, whose interests are being served by the ideology of the biblical text (cf. Exum, 1995b, pp.65–90)?

At this point, it may be salutary to examine in some detail one narrative in the Hebrew Bible where women ostensibly appear to achieve a notable victory within the patriarchal system, but where the suspicious reader may well wonder whether the success supposedly achieved was rather less than satisfactory for the women concerned.

The Case of the Daughters of Zelophehad

The narrative contained in Num. 27:1–11 relates the story of the daughters of Zelophehad, whose father had died without leaving any sons. The daughters appear before Moses, Eleazar the priest and the leaders of the congregation and argue that, in the absence of any male heirs, they should be accorded the right to inherit their father's estate. The case presented by them was evidently so exceptional that Moses had to seek Yahweh's guidance in the matter (v.5), and a decision was rendered acknowledging the legitimacy of their claim (v.7). A formal law was then drafted permitting daughters to inherit the property of their deceased father (vv.8–11a) and the case is said to have set a legal precedent that was henceforth regarded as valid and binding in Israel (v.11b).

This story has frequently been interpreted by feminist scholars as striking a blow in favour of women's rights. Through their persistence and shrewdness,[5] the daughters of Zelophehad demonstrated that, even in a predominantly patriarchal society, women could, if so minded, cause the seemingly rigid structures of ancient Israel's law to be changed or modified. Their petition for an amendment to existing legislation was not only accepted but was given a divine seal of approval, and the daughters were appropriately rewarded for their initiative and resourcefulness by being granted rights and privileges in matters of inheritance that had previously been accorded only to sons. The narrative is thus regarded as one of the rare instances in the Hebrew Bible in which a female voice was heard and in which the grievance of women was recognized and their cause vindicated.

Upon closer inspection, however, it is questionable whether the narrative represents such a victory over patriarchy as is often assumed. In the first place, the daughters are depicted as acting, not for personal gain, but solely in the interests of their deceased father, for they plead to be allowed to inherit his property in order that *his* name might be preserved and that *his* memory might be cherished (v.4).[6] There is no attempt on their part to question the logic behind the law that debarred daughters from sharing in their father's inheritance; their sole concern appears to be that the memory of their father should be perpetuated.

Moreover, although a new law was drafted as a result of their plea (vv.8–11a), the order of precedence in the inheritance of property still gave priority to the male descendants of the deceased: sons were to retain first rights to any inheritance, and only in the absence of a son could the estate pass to a daughter. Thus the petition of the daughters did little to alter the primary aim of the law, which was to preserve the principle of the transference of property according to the male line (cf. Ilan, 2000, p.181). That the patriarchal stake in the inheritance of land was the paramount concern of the legislator is further confirmed by the supplement to this narrative found in Num. 36. It was evidently realized, rather belatedly, that the ruling of Num. 27:8–11a carried a potential hazard: should the daughters marry, there was a risk that the property of their father might pass into the possession of another tribe. Hence an amendment had to be made to the original law to the effect that daughters who inherited their father's estate would be required to marry within their own tribe. Significantly, the narrative in Num. 36 concludes with an account of Zelophehad's daughters dutifully complying with this regulation (vv.10–12): they marry their first cousins on their father's side, thus ensuring that the land would continue to be passed down through their father's tribe.[7]

Once the ideological undercurrents of the narratives concerning the daughters of Zelophehad are brought to the fore, one is left wondering whether their achievement did, in fact, amount to a notable victory for the rights of women. Given the marital constraints that were subsequently imposed upon them, was it really in their interests to have been granted the right to inherit their father's property? Did the success of their appeal not result in further restrictions upon their freedom? Would they not have been able to choose a future spouse more freely if they had not won their case (cf. Sterring, 1994, p.95)? Moreover, the law permitting the daughter to inherit the property of her deceased father did not mean that the territory in question would henceforth be passed down through the maternal line. Rather, it would be inherited by that daughter's son, and then through subsequent male succession. In the patriarchal scheme of things, the inheritance of land by a daughter appears to have been just a temporary anomaly, an aberration that would be corrected once the daughter gave birth to a son. Thus there is a sense in which the daughter, despite the ruling of Num. 27:8–11a, did not 'inherit' property as such; she was merely a conduit to transfer the inheritance from her father to his grandson, thereby facilitating the transfer of property through the male line. The ultimate irony in the case of Zelophehad's daughters is that they end up marrying their cousins from other clans of the tribe of Manasseh, thus ensuring that their father's property passed to those who would have inherited it in any case, even if they had not troubled to stake a claim for the land themselves. Despite the ostensible victory achieved by the daughters, it is the patriarchal principle of lineage, succession and inheritance which triumphed in the end.

Reading against the Grain

Feminist biblical critics are only too aware that readers of the Bible have traditionally succumbed to the ideology of the text and adopted it as their own. They have read 'with the grain' of the text, without pausing to question its underlying values and assumptions. Of course, this is the type of reading of which the biblical authors themselves would have approved, for their aim was to promote their own ideological agendas, and if they succeeded in carrying the reader along with them, so much the better. But reading against the grain of the text means challenging its assumptions and insights and making visible what the text contrives to keep hidden. It means raising issues that the biblical writers did not wish to be raised, and reading the biblical text in a way in which its authors did not intend it to be read.

An example of such a counter-reading of the biblical text may be found in the way in which some feminist biblical scholars have broached the story discussed above (pp.69–70) concerning Jephthah's daughter (Judg. 11:29–40). Traditionally, readers of the text have sympathized with her plight and have admired her indomitable courage and fortitude. As one who showed neither anger nor self-pity, but considered herself as the victim of circumstances beyond her control, she is admired, praised and revered. But to regard her in such a light would be to read 'with the grain' of the text and to view Jephthah's daughter precisely as the biblical author intended us to view her.

However, the dissenting reader, who reads 'against the grain' of the text, would not take such a positive view of Jephthah's daughter; in fact, she would be regarded as culpable for accepting her situation with such composure. Why, for example, did she not challenge the inviolability of the vow?[8] Why did she not seek its annulment instead of merely its postponement? Why did she not rebel against her father and rebuke him for uttering such rash and foolish words? Why did she accept her fate with such equanimity?[9] Why did she display such self-abnegation and abject humility by speaking out as she did in defence of patriarchal authority? Indeed, a dissenting reader would not take quite such a benign view of the activity (or, rather, the lack of activity) of the deity in the narrative. Where was the God who was seemingly indifferent to human suffering? Why did he not intervene to save Jephthah's daughter from her fate, as he intervened to save Isaac from being sacrificed? Instead of accepting the text at face value, the dissenting reader learns to read against the grain of the text and to ask questions that may be unsettling but which force readers to think seriously about the implications of what they are reading.

Occasionally, however, the process of reading 'against the grain' leads the feminist biblical critic not only to question the text's ideology but to resist or even reject it. The strategy invites them to assume a critical, dissociating position from what the text offers and encourages them to articulate their differences with the biblical authors. Of course, there will be times when the reader will be happy to go with the flow of the text and to concur with its value judgments; but there will be other times when its injunctions will be regarded as misguided and its teaching viewed as potentially dangerous or subversive. On such occasions, the reader will want to question and probe the text's values and subject them to critical appraisal, and perhaps even outright rejection.

One aspect of the teaching of the Hebrew Bible which has sometimes called for such a reaction by feminist biblical critics is the use made by the prophets of the marriage metaphor and their application of explicit sexual imagery to depict the relation between Yahweh and Israel (see above, p.6). The breach in the covenant relationship is frequently described in terms of a marriage in which the wife, representing Israel, has constantly been unfaithful to her husband, representing God (cf. Hos. 1–3). The idolatrous nation had acted like a harlot (Hos. 2:5; cf. Bird, 1989, pp.75–94) and therefore deserved to be punished, shamed and disgraced. The punishment inflicted upon her is often described in the most lurid and graphic terms: she will be stripped naked, exposed and publicly humiliated (Hos. 2:3; Jer. 13:20–27); she will be abused, battered and raped (Ezek. 16:6–52; 23:22–49); and she will be derided, mocked and ridiculed (Ezek. 23:32–4). Such retaliation, it is implied, was no more than the wife/nation deserved for betraying the trust of her husband/God by indulging in sexual liaisons with other men. Indeed, in some cases, the wife is regarded as not only responsible for, and guilty of, her own violation but as enjoying the abuse which she was made to suffer (Ezek. 23:5–8, 19–21; cf. Dijk-Hemmes, 1993a, pp.166–7).

Not surprisingly, both the marriage metaphor and the crude sexual imagery which often accompanies it have been roundly condemned by feminist critics. The marriage metaphor is regarded as objectionable because it serves to reinforce the gender hierarchy between male and female by promoting the patriarchal view of marriage as an arrangement in which the husband exercised the dominant role (cf. Exum, 1995a, pp.258–9). It is he who disciplines his wife and who inflicts punishment upon her, and it is to him that she is answerable for her unfaithfulness. Male supremacy in the divine sphere legitimated male supremacy in the human sphere, and the identification of Yahweh with the husband perpetuated the view that power and dominance were essentially a man's prerogative.

Similarly, the sexual imagery deployed by the prophets is criticized because it presents a negative view of female sexuality by implying that women were by nature deviant and promiscuous and that female desire was motivated not by love but by lust (cf. Jer. 2:23–5; Brenner, 1995a, pp.262–4). By suggesting that the punishment which women received at the hands of their husbands was entirely justified, the text gives a divine stamp of approval for the contempt in which they were held and the violence with which they were treated.

Some biblical scholars have sought to play down the significance of such prophetic imagery by emphasizing that the prophets were speaking only of the metaphorical abuse of metaphorical women and that on no account should their words be taken literally (cf. Carroll, 1995, pp.276–9). However, such an argument fails to appreciate the power of metaphor to confirm sexual stereotypes and to reinforce notions of male authority and domination (Weems, 1995, pp.106–19; Graetz, 1995, pp.134–5; Exum, 1995a, pp.263–4). Feminist biblical critics are only too aware of the potentially harmful effects of such imagery on the social standing and self-esteem of women and on gender relations in general. Following the lead of the reader-response critics, the question they are concerned to ask, when faced with such passages in the prophets, is not 'What do these texts mean?' but 'What do these texts *do?*' What effect does reading them have on *real* women who have been victims of sexual or physical abuse? How are females supposed to respond to images which appear to justify violence against women and which luxuriate in the gruesome details of their humiliation (Weems, 1995, pp.8–9, 84–9; Thistlethwaite, 1985, pp.96–107)?

The reaction of the reader was regarded as of paramount importance for feminist biblical critics, for one of their primary aims was to revitalize readers' engagement with the text and make them more conscious of their own response to what they were reading. To ask, simply, 'What does the text say?' was not enough; readers were encouraged to go much further and ask, 'What does the text say to *me?*' and, even more importantly, "What do *I* say to *it?*' (Jauss, 1982, pp.146–7). Am I prepared to tolerate the obscene and offensive language encountered in the prophetic images, or will I recognize them for what they are: 'religious pornography' designed to perpetuate male, sexist propaganda?[10] Am I going to capitulate to the viewpoint of the biblical author or will I resist images that rationalize, eroticize and sensationalize violence against women? Am I going to submit to the ideology of the text or will I reject representations of the female as depraved, shameless and promiscuous? Some feminist biblical scholars have deployed their exegetical skills in an attempt to temper the obscenity of the prophetic passages and to mitigate their damaging effects, but such attempts are often disingenuous and seldom succeed in making the texts more palatable. It is far preferable to face such texts head-on and claim the right to interrogate their values and question their defamatory content.

To deploy such a strategy of resistance to the text is by no means easy, for, as has already been observed (pp.50–52), there is a natural expectation that the reader will assimilate the ideology of the text and identify with the prophet's point of view. But this is precisely why 'reading against the grain' is such an important weapon in the arsenal of feminist critics, for the alternative would be to allow oneself to be co-opted by the text into accepting its ideology uncritically. In the case of the prophetic imagery discussed above this would involve accepting its negative stereotyping of women and viewing their abuse as a normal and inevitable part of human experience.

Ideological Critique and Biblical Authority

The type of strategy advocated above inevitably raises issues concerning the nature of biblical authority, and many will no doubt harbour serious misgivings about the propriety of adopting such an approach to the biblical text. The role of the reader, they would argue, is to submit to the authority of Scripture, not to question or criticize it, and the task of the biblical exegete is to affirm the values enshrined in the biblical text, not to repudiate or reject them. The text of the Bible should be treated with reverential deference, not soiled with ideological probings. For those who hold such a view, the type of approach advocated above will be viewed with grave suspicion, for it will be seen as compromising the very essence of Scripture by reducing the word of God to the level of the human, the social and the ephemeral.

For some feminist biblical scholars such reservations are no more than an irrelevant distraction. They do not read or study the Bible from a religious perspective, and so the question of the Bible's authority is, quite simply, a non-issue. Its writings must be evaluated on the same terms as other writings and its pronouncements must be evaluated on the basis of value systems other than its own. Over against the doctrinal understanding of the divine inspiration of Scripture they would argue, with Elizabeth Cady Stanton, that the Bible bears the imprint of men who never 'saw or talked with God' (1895, p.12). Other feminists claim adherence to the basic tenets of the biblical faith but would want to affirm the importance of female experience over against the authority of Scripture, and would argue that whenever the biblical text falsifies, distorts or denies women's experience it does not have the authority of revelation and does not function as the inspired word of God. Schüssler Fiorenza, for example, argues that a feminist theological interpretation of Scripture must maintain that 'only the nonsexist and non-androcentric traditions of the Bible ... have the theological authority of revelation if the Bible is not to continue as a tool for the oppression of women' (1981, p.106), and she contends that those who regard the patriarchal texts of the Bible as the word of God proclaim him, in effect, as the God of oppression (1984, p.xiii).

The view taken here, however, is that the Hebrew Bible, despite its patriarchal bias, can still be regarded as authoritative for the female reader, for she can appeal to those elements within the biblical tradition that attempt to militate against patriarchal domination. She can question and resist the Bible's patriarchal pronouncements without having to assume a non-confessional stance, for the Hebrew Bible often probes and questions its own values, principles and assumptions. Abraham's plea that the 'judge of all the earth' should 'do what is right' (Gen. 18:25), Job's doubts concerning the essential justice of God, and the Psalmist's question, 'Why do the wicked prosper?' (cf. Ps. 94:3) all belong to a tradition of challenging deeply held assumptions. Such critical questioning is also characteristic of the major prophets, who constantly re-evaluated the traditions which they had inherited as they sought to make them relevant and applicable to their own age. If the traditions were to remain normative and meaningful they had to be critically appraised and had to maintain their value and relevance in the face of critical questioning. The Hebrew canon is the literary deposit of a long critical process in which the biblical authors spoke 'under correction' in their constant striving to make their message applicable (cf. Brett, 1991, pp.25–6). The traditions, therefore, remained subject to continual modification and reformulation in order to take account of changed circumstances.

Now this dialectical process of criticism and renewal of traditions apparent within the Hebrew Bible may be regarded as providing a seal of approval for an ideological critique of Scripture, for there is a sense in which a 'hermeneutic of suspicion' is encountered within the biblical tradition itself as the biblical authors question past beliefs and query past judgments. Far from accepting passively the values which they had inherited, their strategy was to probe, challenge, modify and even reject some of their own inherited traditions. In brief, the Hebrew Bible comes to us bearing clear traces of its own critique of tradition.

It could be argued, therefore, that in applying to the text of the Hebrew Bible a 'hermeneutic of suspicion' feminist criticism merely 'continues the process of Scriptural hermeneutic itself' (Ruether, 1985, p.122). The Hebrew Bible itself provides feminist biblical critics with a warrant to dissent from its teachings and to question its patriarchal assumptions. Indeed, some see the feminist agenda as a natural progression from the prophetic critique of social justice; it is merely that the injustice against which feminists inveigh is that perpetrated against women (cf. Sakenfeld, 1985, p. 55; Ruether, 1985, pp.59–66). Of course, some would quibble with such reasoning, arguing that there is no warrant for extending the Bible's general critique of oppression to a critique of sexism and patriarchy that is not in the biblical text. In response, however, it may be argued that there is an implicit critique of patriarchy in the biblical text, although it may not always be apparent on the surface.

In this regard, Ilana Pardes' examination of the counter-traditions present in the Hebrew Bible (1992) is significant, for she has explored the tensions which exist in the biblical text between the dominant patriarchal ethos and the female counter-voices which lie buried beneath the surface. In a similar vein, Phyllis Trible has drawn attention to the 'depatriarchalizing' principle which is at work in the Hebrew Bible (1973, pp.30–48). Such studies serve as a reminder that the voice of patriarchy is not the only one to be heard in the biblical text and that traces exist within the biblical tradition of the suppressed female voice, although these have usually been overlooked in the writings of male-dominated biblical scholarship. That such traces should be present in the Hebrew Bible should occasion no surprise, for subversive voices can never be fully quelled, and there will always be those who will strive to keep alive aspirations which are diametrically opposed to those of the powerful and dominant in society. Views representing the ideological victors are not the only ones preserved in Scripture, for people will always find ways of effecting change no matter how strong the oppressive structures that militate against them.

It would thus be a gross oversimplification to suggest that there is in the Hebrew Bible a single, unified, coherent ideology; rather, the biblical text is full of ideological ambiguities. Side by side with the ideology that extols obedience to authority, we find one that questions or rejects that authority; side by side with the voice of the oppressor, we hear the cries of the victims of oppression; side by side with the ethos of male domination, we encounter voices of women who struggled within and against the patriarchal system. The task of the feminist critic is to discover, by patient analysis, the various counter-currents and contending philosophies in Scripture and to highlight those elements in the tradition which have been submerged by the dominant ideologies.

Sometimes an anti-patriarchal perspective is signalled clearly in the biblical text, and the attempt to subvert patriarchy is all too obvious. Miriam's protest against the privileged status accorded to Moses, for example, was a blatant attempt to defy the secondary, subservient role into which she had been cast (Num. 12:1–2; cf. Pardes, 1992, pp.6–12). Similarly, Michal's criticism of David for his unseemly behaviour in publicly exposing himself was an attempt to assert her own role and authority as his wife (2 Sam. 6:12–23). Of course, both women were duly punished for having the temerity to challenge accepted roles and to oppose established hierarchies, but the significant element is that the anti-patriarchal perspective has been preserved, against all the odds, in the biblical text.

A further example of anti-patriarchal polemic in the Hebrew Bible may be found in the accusation levelled by Rachel and Leah against their father, Laban (Gen. 31:14–16). They complain that they had been granted no share in the inheritance of their father's estate and that he had exploited them and treated them as though they were 'foreigners'. Such was his greed that he had 'sold' them (an apparent reference to the *môhar*, or 'bride-price') and had spent all the money which he had received. For these reasons the daughters were more than happy to give their blessing to Jacob's plan to leave Laban's household and expressed their willingness to accompany him on his journey.

The sisters' complaint is significant in that it offers a thinly disguised critique of the oppression of women within the patriarchal system (cf. Pardes, 1992, p.69). Their words are a remarkably forthright protest against the exploitative male-dominated structures of their day. The narrative bears witness to a clash of competing interests and provides a further example of the way in which an anti-patriarchal perspective has been preserved in the biblical text, and where sceptical voices are given a hearing (cf. Lapsley, 1998, pp.233–48). Such texts suggest that biblical religion and the feminist cause are not necessarily incompatible, and that feminist critics who struggle to find their voices in a patriarchal religion do so 'in solidarity with the women who went before us' (Plaskow, 1990, pp.51–2).

In the above examples it is not difficult to tease out the anti-patriarchal perspective from the male-oriented text, but in other passages the antithetical undercurrents are much more covert, and in such cases the most effective way of discerning elements in the text which are in conflict with the dominant ideology is the method known as 'deconstruction'. Adherents of this strategy are not interested in viewing the biblical narrative as a coherent, unified whole; their concern, rather, is to root out its ambiguities and to highlight the hidden contradictions within the text. Biblical narratives are viewed as sites of competing interests where several messages may be struggling for precedence, and where dominant and submerged voices are in dynamic tension with one another. By drawing attention to attitudes and viewpoints in the narrative which appear to run against the main drift of the story, deconstructionists aim to reveal the covert and potentially subversive ideology latent in the text. Such a strategy is not without its detractors, but its advantage is that it allows all the voices in the text to be heard and it makes readers more sensitive to the various nuances of meaning which the narratives contain. By analysing the discordant voices, the conflicting messages and the competing claims within a particular narrative, deconstructionists demonstrate that texts sometimes have an uncanny way of contradicting themselves and that they can even undermine the very philosophy which they assert (cf. Culler, 1983, p.86).

Now when this methodology is applied to the Hebrew Bible it becomes evident that some biblical passages, while ostensibly affirming the value of the patriarchal system, manage, at the same time, to disavow the hierarchical ordering of the sexes. Such passages indicate the difficulty of maintaining patriarchy in the face of strong counter-currents which affirmed the role and importance of women. When the biblical text is deconstructed the patriarchal hierarchy breaks down and the ideology of male domination is subverted.

Such a deconstructionist approach has been applied, for example, to the narrative contained in Judg. 1:11–15, which offers a brief account of the offering by Caleb of his daughter Achsah to the man who succeeded in conquering the Canaanite settlement of Kiriath-sepher. Othniel, Caleb's younger brother, accepts the challenge and succeeds in capturing the city, whereupon Caleb honours his commitment and gives Achsah to him as a wife. She urges her husband to ask her father for a field, and finally she confronts her father herself with the request, and her wish is granted.

The portrayal of Achsah in the narrative is ambiguous and contradictory. At the beginning of the story she occupies the passive, subservient role often allotted to women in the Hebrew Bible: as her father's possession, she was liable to be given away as a reward to the warrior who waged a successful military campaign against the enemy. She was merely an incentive for the Israelites to engage in further military expansion, and was viewed as little more than the 'collateral for a piece of Canaanite real estate' (Fewell, 1995, p.134). The fact that she is 'given' implies her subordination to male authority; like the conquered land, she was there to be taken by the victorious warrior. Even her name (meaning 'anklet' or 'bangle') was indicative of her subservient status: she was merely a piece of decoration to be given as the hero's reward.

Once Achsah becomes Othniel's wife, however, she is portrayed rather differently. She now becomes an active participant in the events and urges her husband to ask her father for a plot of land to cultivate. Whether her husband ignored her suggestion, or whether his request to Caleb failed, is not reported, but the story concludes with Achsah herself making the request of her father: 'Give me a present; since you have set me in the land of the Negeb, give me also Gulloth-mayim' (v.15). Her wish is granted, and Caleb gives her Upper Gulloth and Lower Gulloth.

When the text is deconstructed its contradictions and tensions become all too apparent. On the one hand, Achsah appears as a vulnerable woman, whose fate is determined entirely by her father's whim. But the ideology of male dominion breaks down when she demands a piece of property from her father, for she now emerges, not as a subservient daughter, but as an assertive wife. The image of the female as a commodity which could be bartered in exchange for military conquest is suddenly subverted as Achsah begins to assume an active role in the unfolding of events. The passage, although brief, indicates that there are antithetical undercurrents within the biblical text which call into question the repression of the female, and the story provides an example of the way in which traditional sources can yield 'subversive memories' (Schüssler Fiorenza, 1984, pp.19–20) of past struggles against patriarchal domination.

Such texts as those discussed above suggest that, despite the patriarchal emphasis of the Hebrew Bible, the biblical tradition also contains narratives which either overtly reject or implicitly undermine the patriarchal structures which ostensibly appear to dominate the text. There is a tradition of resistance to patriarchal domination within the Bible itself, and feminist biblical critics can therefore claim the authority of biblical faith to denounce its patriarchal agenda (cf. Ruether, 1982, p.55). There is thus a sense in which the 'hermeneutic of suspicion' is not a methodology imposed extraneously upon the biblical text, for its roots may be traced back to the biblical tradition itself.

Gendered Reading

Feminist critics are concerned not only with the patriarchal bias of the biblical text but with the patriarchal bias of its subsequent interpretation.[11] As Schüssler Fiorenza has observed, biblical texts have traditionally been interpreted by, and in the interests of, white middle-class males, usually of European or North American extraction, who have tacitly assumed that theirs is the only legitimate way of reading the Bible (1988, pp.40–43). It is *they* who have assumed the authority to comment upon the biblical text and to control its interpretation, and it is *they* who have decided what sort of questions should be addressed to the Bible and what sort of answers can be regarded as acceptable.

One of the reasons often given for the predominantly male bent of biblical scholarship is that biblical seminaries, divinity schools and theological faculties were traditionally the preserve of male students; women were denied educational opportunities and consequently found it all but impossible to influence the shaping of religious academic discourse. Not only was the biblical literature itself male-dominated but so were the academic institutions in which it was studied. As a result, women found themselves in the unenviable position of being excluded both from the biblical text and from the process of its interpretation. There was a sense in which they were caught in a vicious circle: the subservient role accorded to women in the Bible had resulted (among other things) in their exclusion from theological training, and the effect of that exclusion was that biblical interpretation remained resolutely in the grasp of male commentators and male theologians.

The inequity of such a system was not lost upon the early feminists. For example, in 1878 Mathilda Joslyn Gage, at the annual meeting of the National Woman's Suffrage Association, introduced a resolution which demanded the right of women to interpret Scripture, a right hitherto exercised only by men (cf. Schüssler Fiorenza, 1998, p.60). A similar sentiment was echoed by Frances E. Willard, who complained of the 'one-sided interpretation of the Bible by men' (1889, p.37), and who urged young women of linguistic competence to immerse themselves in Hebrew and New Testament Greek, so that they might interpret the Bible 'in the interest of their sex' (p.31). There was a growing realization among feminists that male-dominated biblical scholarship had resulted in a biased interpretation of Scripture, and that the only way to remedy the situation was for women to demand the right to interpret the Bible from their own perspective.

The matter was stated very plainly by Sarah Moore Grimké, a noted anti-slavery campaigner and women's rights author, who protested vigorously against the 'false translation' of some biblical passages produced by male translators, and who opposed 'the perverted interpretation by the MEN who undertook to write commentaries thereon'. Grimké ventured to suggest, with characteristic understatement, that 'when we are admitted to the honor of studying Greek and Hebrew, we shall produce some various readings of the Bible a little different from those we have now'.[12] Elizabeth Cady Stanton similarly complained that the male bias of the biblical text had been perpetuated by male commentators and male teachers responsible for theological education. Such people were guilty of denigrating the status of women in society: 'Do our sons in their theological seminaries rise from their studies of the Mosaic laws and Paul's epistles with higher respect for their mothers? Alas … they may have learned their first lessons of disrespect and contempt' (1895, p.76). It was just such a deep-seated mistrust of male scholars that provided Cady Stanton with the incentive to produce *The Woman's Bible*, and it is clear from her own contributions to the volume that she was as dismissive of the male bias that had (in her view) distorted the interpretation of the Bible as she was of the implicit misogyny of the biblical text itself.

The reservations concerning the male-centred nature of biblical scholarship adumbrated by the early feminists were echoed by the so-called 'second wave' of feminists in the 1960s. It was their firm conviction that a feminist critique of the biblical text must be matched by a feminist critique of the patriarchal character of the discipline as a whole. Indeed, Schüssler Fiorenza called for nothing short of a 'paradigm shift' in the intellectual framework of the discipline, and she argued that the predominantly androcentric, male-centred world-view should give way to a more inclusive, all-embracing perspective (1984, pp.2–8; 1999, pp.31–81). Of course, feminist biblical scholars were under no illusion that such a shift could easily or quickly be undertaken. Since the biblical authors were (presumably) male and biblical commentators were (predominantly) male, the task of questioning patriarchal interpretations, exposing androcentric assumptions and correcting one-sided reconstructions of the text was inevitably going to be something of an uphill struggle. Yet few doubted that it was a struggle that was well worth the effort, for feminist biblical critics were adamant that such biased exegesis should not go unchallenged. Just as liberation theologians regarded traditional exegesis as deficient because it was produced by the powerful in favour of the powerful, so feminist scholars saw traditional exegesis as deficient because it was produced by men in order to preserve a society based upon the principle of male dominance. In brief, feminist critics were urged to apply a 'hermeneutic of suspicion' not only to the biblical text but to the history of its interpretation.

Once it was realized how male-dominated the interpretative tradition of biblical scholarship was, an increasing emphasis came to be placed upon the importance of reading the Bible 'as a woman'. Although women had read the Bible for countless generations they had not always been reading it deliberately and self-consciously 'as women'. Such a reading, it was argued, could radically alter one's perception or understanding of a text, for, when women brought their own distinctive experiences and insights to bear upon the Bible, its significance would be considerably enriched. Meanings and nuances latent in a given passage could be recovered by a woman's perspective, which might otherwise have remained hidden or ignored.

In emphasizing the importance of reading the Bible 'as a woman', feminist biblical scholars were clearly indebted to the type of approach advocated by the reader-response critics. As has already been noted, reader-response criticism was concerned with differences between various readings of the same text and with the ways in which one's own particular perspective might influence or condition one's understanding. For feminist critics of the Bible, the issue that needed to be addressed was quite straightforward: if readers differ in their approaches to a text, how much of this difference could be attributed to gender? What difference did it make to the interpretation of a text if the reader was a woman (cf. Culler, 1983, pp.43–64)? Indeed, what difference did it make if the reader was a man?

Male interpreters were thus invited to explore the male bias of their exegesis and to consider how their interpretation might have served to consolidate and reinforce patriarchal values. Feminist critics argued that, for the most part, male biblical scholars had shown little awareness that such a bias even existed. They wrote under the guise of a studied neutrality whereas, in fact, they had (albeit perhaps unwittingly) imposed their own interpretative gloss upon the biblical text.

The way in which male biblical scholars have interpreted the biblical text in such a way as to promote their own patriarchal interests is well illustrated in Phyllis Trible's discussion of the account of the creation and fall in Gen. 2–3 (1978, pp.72–143). These chapters have been regarded over the centuries as one of the mainstays of the argument for female inferiority and they are still 'widely adduced as a justification for misogyny' (Bal, 1987, p.104; cf. Millett, 1969, pp.51–4). Yet, despite the ostensibly negative portrayal of woman in this text, Trible feels no inclination to denounce the story or reject it; nor, indeed, does she feel any resentment when reading it or any embarrassment when proclaiming it. The reason for her positive attitude towards the story lies in her conviction that it is not the narrative itself which promotes male domination and female inferiority, but centuries of male-dominated interpretations of the text, interpretations which have become so familiar that they are ingrained in the collective psyche of readers in the Western world. The basic lines of this interpretation of the narrative are familiar enough: God created man first (Gen. 2:7) and woman last (Gen. 2:22), the clear implication being that she must be inferior or subordinate to him; woman was created for the sake of man, as his 'helper', suggesting that she was merely his assistant or attendant (Gen. 2:18); woman was created out of man's rib, a further sign of her derivative, inferior status (Gen. 2:21–2); woman was responsible for tempting man to disobey the divine command, and hence was the cause of human suffering (Gen. 3:6, 16–19); the woman was eventually punished by God, who allowed man to rule over her (Gen. 3:16*b*).

Trible argues that this reading of the story, informed by centuries of patriarchal interpretation, has virtually acquired the 'status of canonicity' (1978, p.73), and that an attempt must be made to read the narrative without the blinkers of male preconceptions. She thus proceeds to refute, one by one, each of the above statements. In the first place, she argues that the story of the Garden of Eden begins with the creation, not of man, but of *hā-ʾādām*, an 'earth creature', formed from the dust of the earth (*hā-ʾᵃdāmâ*; Gen. 2:7). This earth creature, or earthling, was not as yet identified sexually; sexual differentiation took place only when the earth creature 'through divine surgery' (1995, p.12) was made into two separate beings, one female (*ʾiššâ*), the other male (*ʾîš*; Gen. 2:21–4). Man and woman were thus given sexual identities at the same time and not one as a consequence of the other's prior existence. Their creation was, in Trible's words, 'simultaneous, not sequential' (1978, p.98).

Further, the fact that the woman was created as a 'helper' (Gen. 2:18) was not an indication of her inferior status, for the word 'helper' (*ʿêzer*) was often in the Hebrew Bible used of God as the one who sustained and delivered his people (cf. Ex. 18:4; Deut. 33:7; Ps. 121:2; 124:8). Far from implying inferiority, the word, if anything, connoted an element of superiority, although, in the present context, the addition of the expression 'as his [Trible: its] partner' (*kᵉnegdô*) suggested a relationship of mutuality and equality (Trible, 1978, p.90; cf. Bal, 1987, p.115; Otwell, 1977, p.17). The earth creature was therefore given a partner who was neither its superior nor subordinate. Moreover, the woman was created not from the rib of man but from the rib of the sexually undifferentiated earth creature; hence woman is 'no opposite sex, no second sex, no derived sex – in short, no "Adam's rib"' (Trible, 1978, p.102). The notion that woman was solely responsible for the fall is a further misunderstanding of the narrative, for the serpent addresses the woman with the plural verb form (Gen. 3:1–5), implying that the man was also present and that both were seduced into disobeying the divine command. The confessions uttered by the man and woman later in the narrative (Gen. 3:12–13) confirm that 'the image of God male and female has participated in a tragedy of disobedience' (Trible, 1978, p.139). Finally, it is as a result of disobedience that the woman is told that her husband will rule over her; this was not a divine sanction for male supremacy but a description of the corrupt and perverse nature of human life after the expulsion from Eden: 'His supremacy is neither a divine right nor a male prerogative. Her subordination is neither a divine decree nor the female destiny ... God describes this consequence but does not prescribe it as punishment' (Trible, 1978, p.128).

In proposing such a reading of Gen. 2–3, Trible's aim was to 'undercut patriarchal interpretations alien to the text' (1979, p.79). When the narrative is read without any sexist presuppositions, the traditional negative portrayal of Eve is replaced by one which views her in a far more positive light. It is she, after all, who contemplates the tree and appreciates its aesthetic dimensions; it is she who takes the initiative and dares to defy the divine command. Instead of viewing her as gullible, untrustworthy and the embodiment of corruption, she emerges from Trible's reading of the story as alert, perceptive, informed and intelligent (1978, p.110). Moreover, the relation between the couple is shown to be one of mutuality and equality, not one of superiority and subordination, and a story traditionally regarded as imbued with chauvinistic ideas is shown to betray a surprisingly egalitarian concept of the role of the sexes.

Trible's interpretation of Gen. 2–3 is not without its exegetical difficulties (cf. Clines, 1990b, pp.25–48) and it must be conceded that it smacks at times of special pleading. As Ilana Pardes has remarked, in Trible's hands 'the Bible almost turns into a feminist manifesto, where every detail suspiciously ends up supporting woman's liberation' (1992, p.24). Nevertheless, Trible's exegesis of Gen. 2–3 does show how generations of male commentators have imposed their own interpretative gloss on the text, and how a feminist perspective can lead to a different understanding of an all too familiar biblical story. By probing mistranslations and highlighting misconceptions, she has allowed the reader to approach the text from a fresh vantage point and to explore new avenues of meaning in the subtle nuances of its vocabulary. What Trible has done, in effect, is to apply a 'hermeneutic of suspicion' to the traditional patriarchal interpretation of the text, and she has demonstrated how a one-sided view of the story has led male biblical scholars to interpret it as legitimating woman's secondary role and inferior status. The importance of Trible's interpretation is not that it offers a 'correct' reading of the text (whatever that means), but that it offers an alternative reading, and serves to illustrate how one and the same text can authorize a plurality of different interpretations.

Ethical Criticism

Male interpreters of the Bible were guilty of other shortcomings besides imposing their own gender bias upon the biblical text. Sometimes the sin which they committed was one of omission: they had examined the text in detail but had taken no stand with regard to its negative gender implications. They had been quite prepared to question the historical accuracy and reliability of the biblical traditions but had shied away from questioning the validity of its moral norms and underlying assumptions. Consequently, the task of evaluation had been all but evacuated from the realm of biblical scholarship. Male commentators had deployed all the critical tools at their disposal to expound the biblical texts but had stopped short of passing a judgment upon them. In this regard, Cheryl Exum has observed how male commentators, faced with imagery of divine sexual abuse in the prophets (for example, Hos. 2:9–10; Is. 3:16–17; Jer. 13:22), have tended to pass over the moral difficulties occasioned by such representations of the harsh, cruel and vindictive deity, preferring to focus instead on issues of philological or historical–critical import (1995a, pp.260–64). Texts which had served the interests of female oppression, and which should have been exposed, critiqued and evaluated, had been passed over with scarcely a comment. Male commentators had simply reproduced the biblical representations of God as the perpetrator of violence against women without a murmur of protest and without engaging in a serious analysis of the rhetoric of oppression. They had failed to take account of the ethical, social and political consequences of their interpretation, and had appeared to be untroubled and unconcerned by the negative implications of the text which was the object of their study. By failing to question the text's ideology, they had effectively given it their tacit nod of approval; by refraining from commenting upon the Bible's sexual politics, they had implicitly re-endorsed it.

A striking illustration of the failure of male commentators to question the morality of the biblical text may be seen in a fairly random sample of commentaries on Gen. 19.[13] The narrative recounts how two angels in human form visited Sodom, and were invited by Lot to stay in his house overnight (vv.1–3). While they were there, the men of Sodom surrounded the house and threatened to rape the guests (vv.4–5). Lot sought to protect their well-being by offering his own daughters to the angry mob and suggesting that they rape them instead (vv.6–8). Faced with this chilling account, male commentators almost marvel at Lot's willingness to allow his own daughters to be violated rather than permit the homosexual rape of two strangers who happened to be staying under his roof. John Skinner commended him as a 'courageous champion of the obligations of hospitality' and claimed that the action which he took was 'to his credit' (1930, p.307). Bruce Vawter suggested that Lot was 'more sensitive to the duties of hospitality than those of fatherhood', and in case modern readers of the passage be unduly perturbed by Lot's behaviour, he reassuringly informed them that such action 'would not have seemed as shocking to the ancient sense of proprieties as it may seem to our own' (1977, pp.235–6). Indeed, he concluded that there was 'no need to make excuses' for Lot, since he was basically 'a good and not a bad man' (p.236). Von Rad similarly came to Lot's rescue by suggesting that his action in offering his daughters to be raped 'must not be judged simply by our Western ideas' (1972, p.218), and A.S. Herbert rather lamely attempted to exonerate Lot's behaviour by reminding his readers that Lot had, after all, been living in Sodom, where 'a weakening of his moral judgment' may have taken place (1962, p.46). Such examples could easily be multiplied, but the striking element is the reticence of male commentators to pass judgment on Lot's actions. Instead of condemning him for offering his own daughters as rape victims they sympathize with his predicament and point to mitigating circumstances (such as the oriental respect for hospitality) in order to excuse his behaviour. By contrast, feminist scholars who have commented upon this passage have resolutely refused to see Lot in a positive light and they view his regard for the custom of hospitality as a weak and untenable excuse for his outlandish behaviour (cf. Jeansonne, 1990, pp.35–8).

Conclusion

Without doubt, one of the most important contributions of modern feminist biblical scholars has been to question the ideology latent in the biblical text. By applying a 'hermeneutic of suspicion' to the Hebrew Bible and reading 'against the grain' of the text, they invite readers to evaluate its norms, to interrogate its values and to question its underlying assumptions. Of course, such an adversarial reading of the Bible is bound to raise questions concerning the nature of biblical authority, particularly for feminist critics who are also members of the community of faith. The predicament which they face has been well expressed by Francis Watson: 'Can one accept the force of the feminist critique of the biblical texts and still reaffirm their status as holy scripture, or is this an impossible balancing-act?' (1994, p.viii). We have argued that a resisting reading of Scripture does not demand that the reader assume a non-confessional stance towards the Bible, for there are dissenting voices within the biblical tradition itself which oppose the ideology of patriarchal domination. Feminist critics can therefore legitimately claim the authority of biblical faith itself to oppose its patriarchal agenda.

But feminist critics have been concerned not only with the male bias of the biblical text but with the male bias of its subsequent interpretation. They have demonstrated how our apprehension of a given text can change when women bring their own experiences, their own concerns and their own questions to bear upon the text. In doing so they have invited male commentators to question the assumptions on which their interpretation is based, and they have challenged them to view the biblical text from a different perspective.

Notes

1   Plaskow observes that the Hebrew Bible presents itself as the history of the Jewish people but speaks in the voice of only half the Jewish population; hence 'the need for a feminist Judaism begins with hearing silence' (1990, p.1).

2   It should be noted that Schüssler Fiorenza develops a multidimensional model of feminist biblical interpretation, and the fact that her 'hermeneutic of historical reconstruction' is open to question does nothing to detract from the value of some of the other approaches (such as the 'hermeneutic of suspicion') which she favours (see below, pp.89–91).

3   Cf. Cross and Freedman (1955, p.237), Dijk-Hemmes (1994, pp.200–206), Janzen (1994, pp.187–99), Brenner (1985, p.52).

4   The importance of analysing the ideology of the text is clear from Cheryl Exum's two companion articles on the role of women in the birth narrative of Moses (Ex. 1:8–2:10). In her earlier article, published in 1983, Exum celebrated the positive role attributed to women in this text, where they are depicted as wise and resourceful and brave enough to defy oppression. In her later article (1994), however, she conceded that her earlier study was too restrictive, for it lacked an exposé and critique of the ideology that motivated the author to portray women in such a positive light.

5   The shrewdness of the daughters is evident in their insistence that their father was in no way implicated in Korah's revolt (v.3; cf. Num. 16:1–50), lest their plea be interpreted as a similar form of rebellion against the divinely established order (cf. Sterring, 1994, pp.90–1).

6   Sakenfeld (1992, p.50) suggests that the story of Zelophehad's daughters probably survived in tradition only because the basic issue at stake was the preservation of the father's name. On the indissoluble link between the preservation of the family name and possession of the family patrimony, see Davies (1981b, pp.141–2).

7   Cf. Meyers (1988, p.40), who notes that, although females were permitted to inherit property, 'even this breach in the normal pattern is handled in such a way as to preserve the principle of transferring name and property to succeeding generations according to the father's line'.

8   The rabbis report that Jephthah's daughter tried to persuade her father that he could keep his vow without offering her up as a sacrifice, and she cited examples from Israel's history to buttress her case. Jacob had vowed to give a tithe of all that he had to God, yet he never sacrificed any of his children (Gen. 28:20–22), and Hannah had vowed to dedicate her son to God but she did not sacrifice his life in the process (1 Sam. 1:11). See Kramer (1999, p.70).

9   According to the rabbis, far from accepting her destiny with composure, Jephthah's daughter desperately tried to find a way out of her predicament. Her request to go to the mountains to 'bewail her virginity' was viewed by the rabbis as an excuse for her to go to consult the Sanhedrin to see if a different solution could not be found. Cf. Kramer (1999, pp.70–71), Valler (1999, p.61).

10 Setel (1985, pp.86–95) argued that there was a close correspondence between these prophetic texts and modern pornographic depictions of female sexuality. Brenner (1993a, pp.177–93; 1995a, pp.256–74) compares Jer. 2–5 with a modern pornographic novel, Pauline Réage's *Story of O*. Whether it is right to classify the prophetic imagery as 'pornographic' depends, of course, on one's definition of 'pornography', but if one accepts Brenner's view that pornography qualifies as such when erotic imagery contains elements of violence or abuse (1997b, pp.158–63, 171) then the prophetic images are undoubtedly pornographic.

11 Cheryl Exum, for example, insists that 'both the Bible and the history of biblical scholarship stand in need of feminist critique' (1985, p.73), a sentiment echoed by Trible, who argues that the task of the feminist critic is to 'call the Bible and its interpreters to accountability' (1985, p.147).

12 The quotations are taken from S. Grimké's *Letters on the Equality of the Sexes and Other Essays* in the version edited by E.A. Bartlett (1988, p.38). The volume originally appeared in 1838 under the title, *Letters on the Equality of the Sexes, and the Condition of Woman,* Boston: Isaac Knapp.

13 For a discussion of the way in which male commentators have viewed this chapter, see Lerner (1986, pp.172–3), Rashkow (1998, pp.98–102).

Chapter 6

Conclusion

The preceding discussion has drawn on the work of feminist biblical scholars who share a conviction that the Bible, over the centuries, has served to endorse a social system in which women are regarded as subordinate to their male counterparts. For feminist scholars who adhere to the basic principles of the Jewish or Christian faith, the Bible has inevitably proved to be problematic, and it is little wonder that they have sought various ways to counter the negative implications of its patriarchal emphasis. Some have opted to reject the Bible altogether, regarding it as irredeemably patriarchal and as a source of hindrance for women in their struggle for emancipation. Others have favoured a more positive approach, and have argued that the biblical text, once shorn of its androcentric trappings, is not as oppressively patriarchal as is often supposed. In this volume, we have discussed a fairly representative cross-section of approaches advocated by feminist biblical critics, and we have argued that no strategy can be regarded as satisfactory that does not take seriously the ideology of the biblical text. Consequently, the present study has focused on the various literary devices deployed by the biblical authors to reinforce the subjugation of women and to promote their own patriarchal world-view.

Having uncovered the ideology of the text, the next step was to subject it to critical scrutiny. Drawing upon insights from the realm of secular literary theory, it was argued that readers of the Bible must develop strategies of resistance to the text's dominant ideological perspective. They must apply a 'hermeneutic of suspicion' to the biblical text and reserve the right to question, criticize and oppose statements which appear to be blatantly sexist or discriminatory. Instead of being lulled into a state of passive acceptance, they must learn to become 'dissenting readers'.

The type of strategy associated with the dissenting reader need not, of course, be confined to biblical texts which betray an obvious gender bias, for it can be applied to all passages that appear offensive or unacceptable to the modern reader. Those who enter the world of the Hebrew Bible encounter a culture in which slavery and polygamy were accepted as the norm and in which violence, intolerance and hatred of enemies seem to have been the order of the day. Many of its laws appear, by our standards, to be harsh, cruel and vindictive (cf. Deut. 21:18–21). Several of its narratives (such as those which record the massacre of the Canaanites) relate acts of extreme violence and bloodshed, and – to make matters even worse – such acts are often performed at the express command of God himself (cf. Deut. 7:1–6; Josh.

11:16–23). Even the Book of Psalms, so often regarded as the high-water mark of Israel's faith, frequently breathes a spirit of unbridled revenge, and exhibits an attitude of exclusivism and provincialism that smacks of the worst kind of xenophobia. It is precisely because such texts have had a profoundly negative impact and have often been exploited to serve the interests of the oppressor that the type of adversarial reading pioneered by feminist biblical critics must be applied to the Hebrew Bible. Those engaged in reading the biblical text have a right – and an ethical duty – to evaluate its norms and to resist those elements in its teaching that appear to be destructive, harmful or detrimental to human well-being.

It was recognized that such a strategy was bound to raise questions concerning the nature of biblical authority, but it was argued that such a resisting reading of the Hebrew Bible was entirely in keeping with the nature of the biblical tradition itself. The type of adversarial reading advocated by feminist biblical critics can be justified on the grounds that an anti-patriarchal perspective has survived, against all the odds, in the biblical text itself. There is thus a sense in which the 'hermeneutic of suspicion' is not something imposed extraneously upon the Hebrew Bible but is a phenomenon which can be seen to operate within the text of Scripture. To become a dissenting reader of Scripture does not, therefore, require the individual to assume a non-confessional stance; on the contrary, feminist readers of the Hebrew Bible can justifiably claim the authority of biblical faith to denounce its patriarchal features.

It is important to recognize that feminist biblical critics have been concerned to challenge not only the patriarchal ethos of the biblical text but also the patriarchal framework of established biblical scholarship. In this regard, one of the most significant, but frequently overlooked, contributions of feminist biblical scholars has been in the realm of what has been termed 'metacommentary'. Recognizing that the field of biblical studies has in the past been largely dominated by men, they have drawn attention to the 'gendered' character of much of what has passed as objective, neutral, dispassionate interpretation. At the same time, they have explored ways in which a feminist perspective can produce a radically different interpretation of the biblical text by alerting the reader to its encoded messages and to the subtle nuances of meaning that might otherwise have remained hidden or ignored. Of course, feminist critics recognize that it would not be possible, or even desirable, to dispose of gender bias in interpretation; their aim is simply to challenge biblical exegetes to reflect critically upon their own assumptions and to explore as openly and honestly as they can their own interpretative interests.

Such a challenge needs to be taken seriously by the scholarly community, for one of the most difficult and uncomfortable tasks that biblical critics can undertake is to recognize the ideological character of their own interpretation. It is a difficult task because our ideological beliefs are deeply entrenched in our subconscious and form part of the very texture of our lives and the structure of values which we take for granted. It is uncomfortable because biblical scholars are generally loath to admit that their interpretation is coloured by their own interpretative interests and ideologies. Indeed, the very word 'ideology' tends to have a pejorative ring and to evoke a whole range of disparaging resonances. Yet, as feminist biblical scholars remind us, we all have our ideological beliefs and presuppositions, and they cannot conveniently be set to one side as we read a biblical text, nor can they simply be dispensed with at will, as we might discard Father Christmas when we no longer believe in him. Our values, prejudices and presuppositions constitute a permanent feature of our mental landscape and are bound to inform our reading and understanding of the biblical text. The task facing biblical interpreters is to ensure that their ideological values no longer remain hidden or unexamined, but that they be alert to their preconceptions and self-conscious of their presuppositions. In brief, they must undertake a critique not only of the biblical text but of their own ideology. Indeed, they may find that exposing the text's ideology is comparatively easy; the difficulty might be exposing their own.

The unmasking of our own prejudices and preconceptions may well prove to be a wholesome and stimulating exercise. In the first place, it should give us pause for thought before cavalierly rejecting as inferior or illegitimate readings governed by interests other than our own. As feminist critics have emphasized, one of the dangers of the so-called 'objective' approach to the Hebrew Bible is that it tends to privilege a single perspective on the text, and to disparage all interpretations that appear to reflect the interests and concerns of the interpreter. However, once biblical scholars recognize that all interpretations – including their own – are ideological and perspective-ridden, they have no ground for supposing that their own particular exegesis of a text is superior or any more legitimate than those proffered by others. One of the merits of the feminist critical approach to the Bible is that it opposes one-dimensional readings of the biblical text and that it recognizes the validity of a plurality of readings of Scripture.

Further, only by recognizing our own preconceptions can we properly interact with the text, for such interaction demands not only that we challenge the text but that we allow the text to challenge us. But the Bible can only challenge our presuppositions and encourage us to modify our perspective if we are aware of those presuppositions in the first place. The strategy advocated by feminist critics thus encourages a certain flexibility and open-mindedness in those who read the Bible, and allows the text to unsettle their convictions, to alter their perspective and to transform their preconceptions.

Although feminist biblical critics have been primarily concerned with the role accorded to women in the biblical text, it is clear that they have, in the process, opened up a veritable Pandora's Box of issues that demand serious and sustained reflection on the part of biblical scholars. In this volume we have sought to assess their contribution and to provide some indication of the methods which they have deployed and the goals to which they aspire. By engaging in a critique of the patriarchal texts of the Hebrew Bible, feminist biblical critics have provided a critique of the way in which the discipline of biblical studies is currently being pursued. They have invited non-feminist scholars to question and re-examine some of their most fundamental presuppositions, and this volume has been written in the conviction that such an invitation is one which biblical scholars cannot afford to refuse.

Bibliography

Ackerman, S. (2002), 'Why is Miriam also among the Prophets? (And is Zipporah among the Priests?)', *Journal of Biblical Literature,* **121**, pp.47–80.

Alter, R. (1981), *The Art of Biblical Narrative*, London: George Allen and Unwin; New York: Basic Books.

Amit, Y. (1999), *History and Ideology: Introduction to Historiography in the Hebrew Bible* (*The Biblical Seminar* 60), Sheffield: Sheffield Academic Press.

Anderson, J.C. (1991), 'Mapping Feminist Biblical Criticism: The American Scene, 1983–1990', *Critical Review of Books in Religion*, Atlanta: Scholars Press, pp.21–44.

Aschkenasy, N. (1986), *Eve's Journey: Feminine Images in Hebraic Literary Tradition*, Philadelphia: University of Pennsylvania Press.

Bach, A. (ed.) (1990), *The Pleasure of Her Text: Feminist Readings of Biblical and Historical Texts*, Philadelphia: Trinity Press International.

Bach, A. (1993a), 'Reading Allowed: Feminist Biblical Criticism Approaching the Millennium', *Currents in Research: Biblical Studies*, **1**, pp.191–215.

Bach, A. (1993b), 'Good to the Last Drop: Viewing the Sotah (Numbers 5.11–31) as the Glass Half Empty and Wondering How to View it Half Full', in Exum, J. Cheryl and Clines, D.J.A. (eds), pp.26–54 (reprinted in Bach, A. (ed.), 1999, pp.503–22).

Bach, A. (ed.) (1999), *Women in the Hebrew Bible: A Reader*, London and New York: Routledge.

Bal, M. (1987), *Lethal Love: Feminist Literary Readings of Biblical Love Stories*, Bloomington: Indiana University Press.

Bal, M. (1988a), *Death and Dissymmetry: The Politics of Coherence in the Book of Judges*, Chicago: University of Chicago Press.

Bal, M. (1988b), *Murder and Difference: Gender, Genre, and Scholarship on Sisera's Death*, trans. M. Gumpert, Bloomington: Indiana University Press.

Bal, M. (1988c), 'Tricky Thematics', in Exum, J.C. and Bos, J.W.H. (eds), pp.133–55.

Bal, M. (1990), 'Dealing/With/Women: Daughters in the Book of Judges', in Schwartz, R.M. (ed.), pp.16–39.

Bar-Efrat, Shimon (1989), *Narrative Art in the Bible* (*Journal for the Study of the Old Testament Supplement Series* 70), Sheffield: Almond Press.

Barr, J. (2000), *History and Ideology in the Old Testament: Biblical Studies at the End of a Millennium*, Oxford and New York: Oxford University Press.

Barthes, R. (1974), *S/Z*, trans. R. Miller, Oxford: Basil Blackwell.

Barton, J. (1996), *Reading the Old Testament: Method in Biblical Study*, 2nd rev. edn, London: Darton, Longman and Todd.

Bass, D.C. (1982), 'Women's Studies and Biblical Studies: An Historical Perspective', *Journal for the Study of the Old Testament*, **22**, pp.6–12.

Beal, T.K. and Gunn, D.M. (eds) (1997), *Reading Bibles, Writing Bodies: Identity and the Book*, London and New York: Routledge.

Bechtel, L.M. (1991), 'Shame as a Sanction of Social Control in Biblical Israel: Judicial, Political and Social Shaming', *Journal for the Study of the Old Testament*, **49**, pp.47–76.

Bechtel, L.M. (1994), 'What if Dinah is not Raped? (Genesis 34)', *Journal for the Study of the Old Testament*, **62**, pp.19–36.

Bechtel, L.M. (2000), 'Dinah', in Meyers, C. (ed.), pp.69–71.

Bellis, A.O. (2000), 'Feminist Biblical Scholarship', in Meyers, C. (ed.), pp.24–32.

Benedict, R. (1934), *Patterns of Culture*, New York: Houghton Mifflin Company.

Berlin, A. (1982), 'Characterization in Biblical Narrative: David's Wives', *Journal for the Study of the Old Testament*, **23**, pp.69–85.

Berlin, A. (1994), *Poetics and Interpretation of Biblical Narrative*, Sheffield: Almond Press; Winona Lake, Ind.: Eisenbrauns.

Bird, Ph. (1974), 'Images of Women in the Old Testament', in Ruether, R.R. (ed.), pp.41–88 (reprinted in Bird, 1997, pp.13–51).

Bird, Ph. (1987), 'The Place of Women in the Israelite Cultus', in Miller, P.D., Jr., Hanson, P.D. and McBride, S. Dean (eds), *Ancient Israelite Religion: Essays in Honor of Frank Moore Cross*, Philadelphia: Fortress Press, pp.397–419 (reprinted in Bird, 1997, pp.81–102).

Bird, Ph. (1989), '"To Play the Harlot": An Inquiry into an Old Testament Metaphor', in Day, P.L. (ed.), pp.75–94 (reprinted in Bird, 1997, pp.219–36).

Bird, Ph. (1997), *Missing Persons and Mistaken Identities: Women and Gender in Ancient Israel*, Minneapolis: Fortress Press.

Bloom, H. (1975), *Kabbalah and Criticism*, New York: The Seabury Press.

Bloom, H. (with D. Rosenberg) (1990), *The Book of J*, New York: Grove Weidenfeld; London: Faber and Faber.

Bohmbach, K.G. (2000), 'Names and Naming in the Biblical World', in Meyers, C. (ed.), pp.33–9.

Booth, W.C. (1983), *The Rhetoric of Fiction*, 2nd edn, Chicago: University of Chicago Press.

Booth, W.C. (1988), *The Company We Keep: An Ethics of Fiction*, Berkeley: University of California Press.

Bos, J.W.H. (1988), 'Out of the Shadows: Genesis 38; Judges 4:17–22; Ruth 3', in Exum, J.C. and Bos, J.W.H. (eds), pp.37–67.

Brenner, A. (1985), *The Israelite Woman: Social Role and Literary Type in Biblical Narrative*, Sheffield: JSOT Press.

Brenner, A. (1993a), 'On "Jeremiah" and the Poetics of (Prophetic?) Pornography', in Brenner, A. and Dijk-Hemmes, F. van (eds), pp.177–93.

Brenner, A. (ed.) (1993b), *A Feminist Companion to Genesis*, Sheffield: Sheffield Academic Press.

Brenner, A. (1994a), 'On Incest', in Brenner, A. (ed.), 1994c, pp.113–38.

Brenner, A. (1994b), 'An Afterword: The Decalogue – Am I an Addressee?' in Brenner, A. (ed.), 1994c, pp.255–8.

Brenner, A. (ed.) (1994c), *A Feminist Companion to Exodus to Deuteronomy*, Sheffield: Sheffield Academic Press.

Brenner, A. (1995a), 'On Prophetic Propaganda and the Politics of "Love": The Case of Jeremiah', in Brenner, A. (ed.), 1995b, pp.256–74.

Brenner, A. (ed.) (1995b), *A Feminist Companion to the Latter Prophets*, Sheffield: Sheffield Academic Press.

Brenner, A. (ed.) (1995c), *A Feminist Companion to Wisdom Literature*, Sheffield: Sheffield Academic Press.

Brenner, A. (1997a), 'The Hebrew God and his Female Complements', in Beal, T.K. and Gunn, D.M. (eds), pp.56–71.

Brenner, A. (1997b), *The Intercourse of Knowledge: On Gendering Desire and 'Sexuality' in the Hebrew Bible,* Leiden: E.J. Brill.

Brenner, A. (1997c), 'Identifying the Speaker-in-the-Text and the Reader's Location in Prophetic Texts: The Case of Isaiah 50', in Brenner, A. and Fontaine, C. (eds), pp.136–50.

Brenner, A. (ed.) (1998), *Genesis: A Feminist Companion to the Bible,* 2nd series, Sheffield: Sheffield Academic Press.

Brenner, A. (ed.) (1999), *Judges: A Feminist Companion to the Bible*, 2nd series, Sheffield: Sheffield Academic Press.

Brenner, A. (ed.) (2000), *Exodus to Deuteronomy: A Feminist Companion to the Bible*, 2nd series, Sheffield: Sheffield Academic Press.

Brenner, A. and Dijk-Hemmes, F. van (eds) (1993), *On Gendering Texts: Female and Male Voices in the Hebrew Bible*, Leiden: E.J. Brill.

Brenner, A. and Fontaine, C.R. (eds) (1997), *A Feminist Companion to Reading the Bible: Approaches, Methods and Strategies*, Sheffield: Sheffield Academic Press.

Brenner, A. and Fontaine, C.R. (eds) (1998), *Wisdom and Psalms: The Feminist Companion to the Bible*, 2nd series, Sheffield: Sheffield Academic Press.

Brett, M.G. (1991), *Biblical Criticism in Crisis? The Impact of the Canonical Approach on Old Testament Studies*, Cambridge: Cambridge University Press.

Brichto, H.C. (1975), 'The Case of the Sôṭā and a Reconsideration of Biblical "Law"', *Hebrew Union College Annual*, **46**, pp.55–70.

Burns, R.J. (1987), *Has the Lord Indeed Spoken Only Through Moses? A Study of the Biblical Portrait of Miriam (Society of Biblical Literature Dissertation Series* 84), Atlanta: Scholars Press.

Camp, C.V. (1997), 'Woman Wisdom and the Strange Woman: Where is Power to be Found?' in Beal, T.K. and Gunn, D.M. (eds), pp.85–112.

Carroll, R.P. (1990), 'Ideology', in Coggins, R.J. and Houlden, J.L. (eds), pp.309–11.

Carroll, R.P. (1995), 'Desire under the Terebinths: On Pornographic Representation in the Prophets – A Response', in Brenner, A. (ed.), 1995b, pp.275–307.

Christ, C.P. and Plaskow, J. (eds) (1979), *Womanspirit Rising: A Feminist Reader in Religion*, San Francisco: Harper.

Christianson, E.S. (1998), 'Qoheleth the "Old Boy" and Qoheleth the "New Man": Misogyny, the Womb and a Paradox in Ecclesiastes', in Brenner, A. and Fontaine, C.R. (eds), pp.109–36.

Clines, D.J.A. (1978), *The Theme of the Pentateuch* (*Journal for the Study of the Old Testament Supplement Series* 10), Sheffield: JSOT Press.

Clines, D.J.A. (1990a), 'Holistic Interpretation', in Coggins, R.J. and Houlden, J.L. (eds), pp.292–5.

Clines, D.J.A. (1990b), *What Does Eve Do to Help? And Other Readerly Questions to the Old Testament* (*Journal for the Study of the Old Testament Supplement Series* 94), Sheffield: Sheffield Academic Press.

Clines, D.J.A. (1991), 'The Story of Michal, Wife of David, in its Sequential Unfolding', in Clines, D.J.A. and Eskenazi, T.C. (eds), pp.129–40.

Clines, D.J.A. (1995), *Interested Parties: The Ideology of Writers and Readers of the Hebrew Bible* (*Journal for the Study of the Old Testament Supplement Series* 205), Sheffield: Sheffield Academic Press.

Clines, D.J.A. (1997), *The Bible and the Modern World* (*The Biblical Seminar* 51), Sheffield: Sheffield Academic Press.

Clines, D.J.A. and Eskenazi, T.C. (eds) (1991), *Telling Queen Michal's Story: An Experiment in Comparative Interpretation* (*Journal for the Study of the Old Testament Supplement Series* 119), Sheffield: Sheffield Academic Press.

Coggins, R.J. and Houlden, J.L. (eds) (1990), *A Dictionary of Biblical Interpretation*, London: SCM; Philadelphia: Trinity Press International.

Collins, A.Y. (ed.) (1985), *Feminist Perspectives on Biblical Scholarship*, Chico, California: Scholars Press.

Cross, F.M. and Freedman, D.N. (1955), 'The Song of Miriam', *Journal of Near Eastern Studies*, **14**, pp.237–50.

Culler, J. (1983), *On Deconstruction: Theory and Criticism after Structuralism*, London: Routledge and Kegan Paul.

Daly, M. (1968), *The Church and the Second Sex,* Boston: Beacon Press.

Daly, M. (1973), *Beyond God the Father: Toward a Philosophy of Women's Liberation*, Boston: Beacon Press.

Darr, K. (1994), *Isaiah's Vision and the Family of God*, Louisville: Westminster/John Knox Press.

Davies, E.W. (1981a), *Prophecy and Ethics: Isaiah and the Ethical Traditions of Israel* (*Journal for the Study of the Old Testament Supplement Series* 16), Sheffield: JSOT Press.

Davies, E.W. (1981b), 'Inheritance Rights and the Hebrew Levirate Marriage', *Vetus Testamentum*, **31**, pp.138–44, 257–68.

Davies, E.W. (1989), 'Land: Its Rights and Privileges', in Clements, R.E. (ed.), *The World of Ancient Israel: Social, Anthropological and Political Perspectives,* Cambridge: Cambridge University Press, pp.349–69.

Davies, E.W. (1995), *Numbers (New Century Bible Commentary)*, London: Marshall Pickering; Grand Rapids: W.B. Eerdmans Publishing Company.

Davies, E.W. (2003), 'Reader-response Criticism and the Hebrew Bible', in Pope, R. (ed.), *Honouring the Past and Shaping the Future: Religious and Biblical Studies in Wales*, Leominster: Gracewing, pp.20–37.

Day, P.L. (ed.) (1989), *Gender and Difference in Ancient Israel*, Minneapolis: Fortress Press.

Dijk-Hemmes, F. van (1993a), 'The Metaphorization of Woman in Prophetic Speech: An Analysis of Ezekiel XXIII', *Vetus Testamentum*, **43**, pp.162–70 (reprinted in Brenner, A. (ed.), 1995b, pp.244–55).

Dijk-Hemmes, F. van (1993b), 'Traces of Women's Texts in the Hebrew Bible', in Brenner, A. and Dijk-Hemmes, F. van (eds), pp.17–109.

Dijk-Hemmes, F. van (1994), 'Some Recent Views on the Presentation of the Song of Miriam', in Brenner, A. (ed.), 1994c, pp.200–206.

Eagleton, T. (1978), *Criticism and Ideology: A Study in Marxist Literary Theory,* London: Verso.

Eagleton, T. (1983), *Literary Theory: An Introduction*, Oxford: Basil Blackwell; Minneapolis: University of Minnesota Press.

Eco, U. (1981), *The Role of the Reader: Explorations in the Semiotics of Texts*, London: Hutchinson and Co.

Eliot, T.S. (1932), *Selected Essays*, London: Faber and Faber.

Exum, J. Cheryl (1980), 'Promise and Fulfillment: Narrative Art in Judges 13', *Journal of Biblical Literature*, **99**, pp.43–59.

Exum, J. Cheryl (1983), '"You Shall Let Every Daughter Live": A Study of Exodus 1.8–2.10', in Tolbert, M.A. (ed.), 1983b, pp.63–82 (reprinted in Brenner, A. (ed.), 1994c, pp.37–61).

Exum, J. Cheryl (1985), '"Mother in Israel": A Familiar Figure Reconsidered', in Russell, L.M. (ed.), 1985b, pp.73–85.

Exum, J. Cheryl (1990), 'Murder They Wrote: Ideology and the Manipulation of Female Presence in Biblical Narrative', in Bach, A. (ed.), pp.45–67.

Exum, J. Cheryl (1992), *Tragedy and Biblical Narrative: Arrows of the Almighty*, Cambridge: Cambridge University Press.

Exum, J. Cheryl (1993), *Fragmented Women: Feminist (Sub)versions of Biblical Narratives (Journal for the Study of the Old Testament Supplement Series* 163), Sheffield: Sheffield Academic Press; Philadelphia: Trinity Press International.

Exum, J. Cheryl (1994), 'Second Thoughts about Secondary Characters: Women in Exodus 1.8–2.10', in Brenner, A. (ed.), 1994c, pp.75–87.

Exum, J. Cheryl (1995a), 'The Ethics of Biblical Violence against Women', in Rogerson, J.W., Davies, M. and Carroll, M.D. (eds), *The Bible in Ethics: The Second Sheffield Colloquium* (*Journal for the Study of the Old Testament Supplement Series* 207), Sheffield: Sheffield Academic Press, pp.248–71.

Exum, J. Cheryl (1995b), 'Feminist Criticism: Whose Interests are being Served?', in Yee, G.A. (ed.), pp.65–90.

Exum, J. Cheryl (2000), 'Feminist Study of the Old Testament', in Mayes, A.D.H. (ed.), *Text in Context: Essays by Members of the Society of Old Testament Study,* Oxford: Oxford University Press, pp.86–115.

Exum, J. Cheryl and Bos, J.W.H. (eds) (1988), *Reasoning with the Foxes: Female Wit in a World of Male Power* (*Semeia*, **42**), Atlanta: Scholars Press.

Exum, J. Cheryl and Clines, D.J.A. (eds) (1993), *The New Literary Criticism and the Hebrew Bible* (*Journal for the Study of the Old Testament Supplement Series* 143), Sheffield: Sheffield Academic Press.

Fetterley, J. (1978), *The Resisting Reader: A Feminist Approach to American Fiction,* Bloomington and London: Indiana University Press.

Fewell, D.N. (1987), 'Feminist Reading of the Hebrew Bible: Affirmation, Resistance and Transformation', *Journal for the Study of the Old Testament*, **39**, pp.77–87.

Fewell, D.N. (1995), 'Deconstructive Criticism: Achsah and the (E)razed City of Writing', in Yee, G.A. (ed.), 1995b, pp.119–45.

Fewell, D.N. (1998), 'Changing the Subject: Retelling the Story of Hagar the Egyptian', in Brenner, A. (ed.), pp.182–94.

Fewell, D.N. and Gunn, D.M. (1991), 'Tipping the Balance: Sternberg's Reader and the Rape of Dinah', *Journal of Biblical Literature*, **110**, pp.193–211.

Fewell, D.N. and Gunn, D.M. (1993), *Gender, Power, and Promise: The Subject of the Bible's First Story*, Nashville: Abingdon Press.

Fewell, D.N. and Gunn, D.M. (1997), 'Shifting the Blame: God in the Garden', in Beal, T.K. and Gunn, D.M. (eds), pp.16–33.

Fish, S.E. (1972), *Self-Consuming Artifacts: The Experience of Seventeenth-Century Literature*, Berkeley and London: University of California Press.

Fish, S.E. (1980), *Is There a Text in this Class? The Authority of Interpretive Communities*, Cambridge, MA, and London: Harvard University Press.

Fontaine, C.R. (1989), 'Hosea', in Anderson, B.W. (ed.), *The Books of the Bible*, New York: Charles Scribner's Sons, pp.349–58 (reprinted in Brenner, A. (ed.), 1995b, pp.40–59).

Fontaine, C.R. (1992), 'Proverbs', in Newsom, C.A. and Ringe, Sharon H. (eds), pp.145–52.

Fontaine, C.R. (1995), 'A Response to "Hosea"', in Brenner, A. (ed.), 1995b, pp.60–69.

Fontaine, C.R. (1997), 'The Abusive Bible: On the Use of Feminist Method in Pastoral Contexts', in Brenner, A. and Fontaine, C.R. (eds), pp.84–113.

Fontaine, C.R. (1998), '"Many Devices" (Qoheleth 7:23–8:1): Qoheleth, Misogyny and the *Malleus Maleficarum*', in Brenner, A. and Fontaine, C.R. (eds), pp.137–68.

Fowler, R.M. (1991), *Let the Reader Understand: Reader-Response Criticism and the Gospel of Mark*, Minneapolis: Fortress Press.

Fox, M.V. (1989), *Qohelet and his Contradictions (Journal for the Study of the Old Testament Supplement Series* 71), Sheffield: Almond Press.

Frymer-Kensky, T. (1984), 'The Strange Case of the Suspected Sotah (Num V 11–31)', *Vetus Testamentum*, **34**, pp.11–26.

Frymer-Kensky, T. (1989), 'Law and Philosophy: The Case of Sex in the Bible', in Patrick, D. (ed.), *Thinking Biblical Law (Semeia*, **45**), pp.89–102.

Frymer-Kensky, T. (1992), 'Deuteronomy', in Newsom, C.A. and Ringe, Sharon H. (eds), pp.52–62.

Frymer-Kensky, T. (1998), 'Virginity in the Bible', in Matthews, V.H., Levinson, B.M. and Frymer-Kensky, T. (eds), pp.79–96.

Fuchs, E. (1985), 'Who is Hiding the Truth? Deceptive Women and Biblical Androcentrism', in Collins, A.Y. (ed.), pp.137–44.

Fuchs, E. (1988), '"For I Have the Way of Women": Deception, Gender and Ideology in Biblical Narrative', in Exum, J. Cheryl and Bos, J.W.H. (eds), pp.68–83.

Fuchs, E. (2000), *Sexual Politics in the Biblical Narrative: Reading the Hebrew Bible as a Woman (Journal for the Study of the Old Testament Supplement Series* 310), Sheffield: Sheffield Academic Press.

Garbini, G. (1988), *History and Ideology in Ancient Israel*, London: SCM Press.

Gifford, C. de Swarte (1985), 'American Women and the Bible: The Nature of Woman as a Hermeneutical Issue', in Collins, A.Y. (ed.), pp.11–33.

Graetz, N. (1993), 'Dinah the Daughter', in Brenner, A. (ed.), 1993b, pp.306–17.

Graetz, N. (1994), 'Did Miriam Talk Too Much?', in Brenner, A. (ed.), 1994c, pp.231–42.

Graetz, N. (1995), 'God is to Israel as Husband is to Wife: The Metaphoric Battering of Hosea's Wife', in Brenner, A. (ed.), 1995b, pp.126–45.

Grimké, S. (1838), *Letters on the Equality of the Sexes, and the Condition of Woman*, Boston: Isaac Knapp.

Gruber, M.I. (1983), 'The Motherhood of God in Second Isaiah', *Revue Biblique*, **90**, pp.351–9 (reprinted in Gruber, M.I., *The Motherhood of God and Other Studies*, Atlanta: Scholars Press, 1992, pp.3–15).

Habermas, J. (1981), 'Ideology', in Bottomore, T. (ed.), *Modern Interpretations of Marx*, Oxford: Basil Blackwell, pp.155–69.

Hackett, J.A. (1985), 'In the Days of Jael: Reclaiming the History of Women in Ancient Israel', in Atkinson, C.W., Buchanan, C.H. and Miles, M.R. (eds), *Immaculate and Powerful: The Female in Sacred Image and Social Reality*, Boston: Beacon Press, pp.15–38.

Hackett, J.A. (1987), 'Women's Studies and the Hebrew Bible', in Friedman, R.E. and Williamson, H.G.M. (eds), *The Future of Biblical Studies: The Hebrew Scriptures,* Atlanta: Scholars Press, pp.141–64.

Hackett, J.A. (1992), '1 and 2 Samuel', in Newsom, C.A. and Ringe, Sharon H. (eds), pp.85–95.

Hammond, G. (1992), 'Michal, Tamar, Abigail and what Bathsheba said: Notes Towards a Really Inclusive Translation of the Bible', in Brooke, G.J. (ed.), *Women in the Biblical Tradition*, Lampeter: The Edwin Mellen Press, pp.53–70.

Hampson, D. (1985), 'The Challenge of Feminism to Christianity', *Theology*, **88**, pp.341–50.

Hampson, D. (1990), *Theology and Feminism*, Oxford: Basil Blackwell.

Herbert, A.S. (1962), *Genesis 12–50*, London: SCM.

Herskovits, M.J. (1972), *Cultural Relativism: Perspectives in Cultural Pluralism*, New York: Random House.

Holland, N.N. (1975), *5 Readers Reading*, New Haven and London: Yale University Press.

Ilan, T. (1993), 'Biblical Women's Names in the Apocryphal Traditions', *Journal for the Study of the Pseudepigrapha*, **11**, pp.3–67.

Ilan, T. (2000), 'The Daughters of Zelophehad and Women's Inheritance: The Biblical Injunction and its Outcome', in Brenner, A. (ed.), pp.176–86.

Iser, W. (1972), 'The Reading Process: A Phenomenological Approach', *New Literary History*, **3**, pp.279–99.

Iser, W. (1974), *The Implied Reader: Patterns of Communication in Prose Fiction from Bunyan to Beckett*, Baltimore: The Johns Hopkins University Press.

Iser, W. (1978), *The Act of Reading: A Theory of Aesthetic Response*, Baltimore and London: The Johns Hopkins University Press.

Iser, W. (1980), 'Interaction between Text and Reader', in Suleiman, S.R. and Crosman, I. (eds), pp.106–19.

Jameson, F. (1981), *The Political Unconscious: Narrative as a Socially Symbolic Act,* London: Methuen; New York: Cornell University Press.

Janzen, J.G. (1994), 'Song of Moses, Song of Miriam: Who is Seconding Whom?', in Brenner, A. (ed.), 1994c, pp.187–99.

Japhet, S. (1997), *The Ideology of the Book of Chronicles and its Place in Biblical Thought*, 2nd rev. edn, trans. A. Barber, Frankfurt and New York: Peter Lang.

Jauss, H.R. (1982), *Toward an Aesthetic of Reception*, trans. T. Bahti, Minneapolis: University of Minnesota Press.

Jeansonne, Sharon P. (1990), *The Women of Genesis: From Sarah to Potiphar's Wife*, Minneapolis: Fortress Press.

Jobling, D. (ed.) (1992), *Ideological Criticism of Biblical Texts* (*Semeia*, **59**), Atlanta: Scholars Press.

Joyce, P. (1990), 'Feminist Exegesis of the Old Testament: Some Critical Reflections', in Soskice, J.M. (ed.), *After Eve: Women, Theology and the Christian Tradition*, London: Marshall Pickering, pp.1–9.

Klein, L.R. (1995), 'Job and the Womb: Text about Men, Subtext about Women', in Brenner, A. (ed.), 1995c, pp.186–200.

Kramer, Ph.S. (1999), 'Jephthah's Daughter: A Thematic Approach to the Narrative as Seen in Selected Rabbinic Exegesis and in Artwork', in Brenner, A. (ed.), pp.67–92.

Lapsley, J.E. (1998), 'The Voice of Rachel: Resistance and Polyphony in Genesis 31.14–35', in Brenner, A. (ed.), pp.233–48.

Lerner, G. (1986), *The Creation of Patriarchy*, Oxford and New York: Oxford University Press.

Loades, A. (1991), 'Beyond God the Father: An Introduction to Mary Daly's View of Christian Tradition', in Linzey, A. and Wexler, P. (eds), *Fundamentalism and Tolerance: An Agenda for Theology and Society*, London: Bellow Publishing, pp.113–22.

Loades, A. (1998), 'Feminist Interpretation', in Barton, J. (ed.), *The Cambridge Companion to Biblical Interpretation*, Cambridge: Cambridge University Press, pp.81–94.

Maertens, T. (1969), *The Advancing Dignity of Woman in the Bible*, trans. S. Dibbs, De Pere, Wisconsin: St. Norbert Abbey Press.

Maier, C. (1995), *Die 'fremde Frau' in Proverbien 1-9: Eine exegetische und sozialgeschichtliche Studie* (*Orbis biblicus et orientalis* 144), Göttingen: Vandenhoeck and Ruprecht.

Maier, C. (1998), 'Conflicting Attractions: Parental Wisdom and the "Strange Woman" in Proverbs 1-9', in Brenner, A. and Fontaine, C.R. (eds), pp.92–108.

Marcus, D. (1986), *Jephthah and his Vow*, Texas: Texas Tech Press.

Matthews, V.H., Levinson, B.M. and Frymer-Kensky, T. (1998), *Gender and Law in the Hebrew Bible and the Ancient Near East* (*Journal for the Study of the Old Testament Supplement Series* 262), Sheffield: Sheffield Academic Press.

McKeating, H. (1979), 'Sanctions against Adultery in Ancient Israelite Society, with some Reflections on Methodology in the Study of Old Testament Ethics', *Journal for the Study of the Old Testament*, **11**, pp.57–72.

Meyers, C. (1983), 'Procreation, Production, and Protection: Male–Female Balance in Early Israel', *Journal of the American Academy of Religion*, **51**, pp.569–93.

Meyers, C. (1988), *Discovering Eve: Ancient Israelite Women in Context*, Oxford and New York: Oxford University Press.

Meyers, C. (1992), 'Everyday Life: Women in the Period of the Hebrew Bible', in Newsom, C.A. and Ringe, Sharon H. (eds), pp.244–51.

Meyers, C. (ed.) (2000), *Women in Scripture: A Dictionary of Named and Unnamed Women in the Hebrew Bible, the Apocryphal/Deuterocanonical Books, and the New Testament*, Grand Rapids, Michigan, and Cambridge, UK: W.B. Eerdmans Publishing Company.

Middleton, D.F. (1990), 'Feminist Interpretation', in Coggins, R.J. and Houlden, J.L. (eds), pp.231–34.

Miller, J. Hillis (1987), *The Ethics of Reading: Kant, de Man, Eliot, Trollope, James, and Benjamin*, New York: Columbia University Press.

Miller, J.M. (1967), 'The Fall of the House of Ahab', *Vetus Testamentum*, **17**, pp.307–24.

Miller, P.D., Jr. (1976), 'Faith and Ideology in the Old Testament', in Cross, F.M., Lemke, W.E. and Miller, P.D. (Jr.) (eds), *Magnalia Dei. The Mighty Acts of God: Essays on the Bible and Archaeology in Memory of G. Ernest Wright*, Garden City, New York: Doubleday, pp.464–79.

Millett, K. (1969), *Sexual Politics*, London: Virago Press; New York: Ballantine Books.

Mills, S. (1994), 'Reading as/like a Feminist', in Mills, S. (ed.), *Gendering the Reader*, London and New York: Harvester Wheatsheaf, pp.25–46.

Milne, P.J. (1995), 'No Promised Land: Rejecting the Authority of the Bible', in Shanks, H. (ed.), pp.47–73.

Milne, P.J. (1997), 'Toward Feminist Companionship: The Future of Feminist Biblical Studies and Feminism', in Brenner, A. and Fontaine, C.R. (eds), pp.39–60.

Morgan, R. and Barton, J. (1988), *Biblical Interpretation*, Oxford: Oxford University Press.

Newsom, C.A. and Ringe, Sharon H. (eds) (1992), *The Women's Bible Commentary*, London: SPCK; Louisville: Westminster/John Knox Press.

Niditch, S. (1992), 'Genesis', in Newsom, C.A. and Ringe, Sharon H. (eds), pp.10–25.

O'Connell, R.H. (1996), *The Rhetoric of the Book of Judges* (*Supplements to Vetus Testamentum* 63), London, New York, Cologne: E.J. Brill.

Ostriker, A.S. (1993), *Feminist Revision and the Bible*, Oxford: Basil Blackwell.

Otwell, J.H. (1977), *And Sarah Laughed: The Status of Woman in the Old Testament*, Philadelphia: Westminster Press.

Pardes, I. (1992), *Countertraditions in the Bible: A Feminist Approach*, Cambridge, MA, and London: Harvard University Press.

Penchansky, D. (2000), 'Job's Wife: The Satan's Handmaid', in Penchansky, D. and Redditt, P.L. (eds), *Shall Not the Judge of All the Earth Do What Is Right?: Studies on the Nature of God in Tribute to James L. Crenshaw*, Winona Lake: Eisenbrauns, pp.223–8.

Pippin, T. (1996), 'Ideology, Ideological Criticism, and the Bible', *Currents in Research: Biblical Studies*, **4**, pp.51–78.

Plaskow, J. (1990), *Standing Again at Sinai: Judaism from a Feminist Perspective*, San Francisco: Harper and Row.

Porter, J.R. (1954), 'The Interpretation of 2 Samuel VI and Psalm CXXXII', *Journal of Theological Studies*, **5**, pp.161–73.

Pressler, C. (1993), *The View of Women Found in the Deuteronomic Family Laws* (*Beihefte zur Zeitschrift für die alttestamentliche Wissenschaft* 216), Berlin and New York: Walter de Gruyter.

Pressler, C. (1994), 'Sexual Violence and Deuteronomic Law', in Brenner, A. (ed.), 1994c, pp.102–12.

Pritchard, J.B. (ed.) (1955), *Ancient Near Eastern Texts Relating to the Old Testament*, 2nd edn, Princeton: Princeton University Press.

Prouser, O.H. (1994), 'The Truth about Women and Lying', *Journal for the Study of the Old Testament*, **61**, pp.15–28.

Provan, I.W. (1995), 'Ideologies, Literary and Critical: Reflections on Recent Writing on the History of Israel', *Journal of Biblical Literature*, **114**, pp.585–606.

Rad, G. von (1972), *Genesis: A Commentary (Old Testament Library)*, 3rd rev. edn, trans. J.H. Marks, London: SCM; Philadelphia: Westminster Press.

Ransom, J.C. (1941), *The New Criticism,* Norfolk, CT: New Directions.

Rashkow, I.N. (1994), 'Daughters and Fathers in Genesis ... Or, What is Wrong with this Picture?', in Brenner, A. (ed.), 1994c, pp.22–36.

Rashkow, I.N. (1998), 'Daddy-Dearest and the "Invisible Spirit of Wine"', in Brenner, A. (ed.), 1998, pp.82–107.

Reinhartz, A. (1992), 'Samson's Mother: An Unnamed Protagonist', *Journal for the Study of the Old Testament*, **55**, pp.25–37.

Reinhartz, A. (1998), *"Why ask my Name?" Anonymity and Identity in Biblical Narrative*, Oxford and New York: Oxford University Press.

Richards, I.A. (1924), *Principles of Literary Criticism*, London: Kegan Paul.

Rofé, A. (1988), 'The Vineyard of Naboth: The Origin and Message of the Story', *Vetus Testamentum*, **38**, pp.89–104.

Ruether, R.R. (ed.) (1974), *Religion and Sexism: Images of Woman in the Jewish and Christian Traditions,* New York: Simon and Schuster.

Ruether, R.R. (1975), *New Woman New Earth: Sexist Ideologies and Human Liberation*, New York: The Seabury Press.

Ruether, R.R. (1982), 'Feminism and Patriarchal Religion: Principles of Ideological Critique of the Bible', *Journal for the Study of the Old Testament*, **22**, pp.54–66.

Ruether, R.R. (1985), 'Feminist Interpretation: A Method of Correlation', in Russell, L.M. (ed.), 1985b, pp.111–24.

Russell, L.M. (1985a), 'Authority and the Challenge of Feminist Interpretation', in Russell, L.M. (ed.), 1985b, pp.137–46.

Russell, L.M. (ed.) (1985b), *Feminist Interpretation of the Bible*, Philadelphia: Westminster Press.

Sakenfeld, K.D. (1982), 'Old Testament Perspectives: Methodological Issues', *Journal for the Study of the Old Testament*, **22**, pp.13–20.

Sakenfeld, K.D. (1985), 'Feminist Uses of Biblical Materials', in Russell, L.M. (ed.), 1985b, pp.55–64.

Sakenfeld, K.D. (1992), 'Numbers', in Newsom, C.A. and Ringe, Sharon H. (eds), 1992, pp.45–51.

Sakenfeld, K.D. (1993), 'Feminism and the Bible', in Metzger, B.M. and Coogan, M.D. (eds), *The Oxford Companion to the Bible*, Oxford: Oxford University Press, pp.228–31.

Sawyer, J.F.A. (1996), *The Fifth Gospel: Isaiah in the History of Christianity*, Cambridge: Cambridge University Press.

Schottroff, L., Schroer, S. and Wacker, M.-T. (1998), *Feminist Interpretation: The Bible in Women's Perspective*, trans. M. and B. Rumscheidt, Minneapolis: Fortress Press.

Schroer, S. (1998), 'Toward a Feminist Reconstruction of the History of Israel', in Schottroff, L., Schroer, S. and Wacker, M.-T. (eds), pp.85–176.

Schüngel-Straumann, H. (1986), 'Gott als Mutter in Hos. 11', *Tübinger Theologische Quartalschrift,* **166**, pp.119–34 (reprinted as 'God as Mother in Hosea 11', in Brenner, A. (ed.), 1995b, pp.194–218).

Schüssler Fiorenza, E. (1979), 'Women in the Early Christian Movement', in Christ, C.P. and Plaskow, J. (eds), pp.84–92.

Schüssler Fiorenza, E. (1981), 'Toward a Feminist Biblical Hermeneutics: Biblical Interpretation and Liberation Theology', in Mahan, B. and Richesin, L.D. (eds), *The Challenge of Liberation Theology: A First World Response*, New York: Orbis Books, pp.91–112.

Schüssler Fiorenza, E. (1982), 'Feminist Theology and New Testament Interpretation', *Journal for the Study of the Old Testament*, **22**, pp.32–46.

Schüssler Fiorenza, E. (1983), *In Memory of Her: A Feminist Theological Reconstruction of Christian Origins*, New York: Crossroad Publishing Company.

Schüssler Fiorenza, E. (1984), *Bread Not Stone: The Challenge of Feminist Biblical Interpretation*, Edinburgh: T. and T. Clark; Boston: Beacon Press.

Schüssler Fiorenza, E. (1985), 'The Will to Choose or to Reject: Continuing our Critical Work', in Russell, L.M. (ed.), 1985b, pp.125–36.

Schüssler Fiorenza, E. (1988), 'The Ethics of Biblical Interpretation: Decentering Biblical Scholarship', *Journal of Biblical Literature*, **107**, pp.3–17.

Schüssler Fiorenza, E. (1993a), *Discipleship of Equals: A Critical Feminist Ekklesialogy of Liberation*, New York: Crossroad Publishing Company.

Schüssler Fiorenza, E. (1993b), 'Transforming the Legacy of *The Woman's Bible',* in Schüssler Fiorenza, E. (ed.), 1993c, pp.1–24.

Schüssler Fiorenza, E. (ed.) (1993c), *Searching the Scriptures. Volume One: A Feminist Introduction*, London: SCM Press; New York: Crossroad Publishing Company.

Schüssler Fiorenza, E. (1998), *Sharing Her Word: Feminist Biblical Interpretation in Context*, Boston: Beacon Press.

Schüssler Fiorenza, E. (1999), *Rhetoric and Ethic: The Politics of Biblical Studies*, Minneapolis: Fortress Press.

Schwartz, R.M. (ed.) (1990), *The Book and the Text: The Bible and Literary Theory*, Oxford: Basil Blackwell.

Scroggs, R. (1972), 'Paul and the Eschatological Woman', *Journal of the American Academy of Religion*, **40**, pp.283–303.

Setel, T.D. (1985), 'Prophets and Pornography: Female Sexual Imagery in Hosea', in Russell, L.M. (ed.), 1985b, pp.86–95.

Shanks, H. (ed.) (1995), *Feminist Approaches to the Bible*, Washington, DC: Biblical Archaeology Society.

Sherwood, Y. (1995), 'Boxing Gomer: Controlling the Deviant Woman in Hosea 1–3', in Brenner, A. (ed.), 1995b, pp.101–25.

Sherwood, Y. (1996), *The Prostitute and the Prophet: Hosea's Marriage in Literary-Theoretical Perspective* (*Journal for the Study of the Old Testament Supplement Series* 212), Sheffield: Sheffield Academic Press.

Shields, M.E. (1995), 'Circumcision of the Prostitute: Gender, Sexuality, and the Call to Repentance in Jeremiah 3:1-4:4', *Biblical Interpretation*, **3**, pp.61–74.

Siebert-Hommes, J. (1994), 'But if she be a daughter ... she may live! "Daughters" and "Sons" in Exodus 1–2', in Brenner, A. (ed.), 1994c, pp.62–74.

Skinner, J. (1930), *A Critical and Exegetical Commentary on Genesis* (*International Critical Commentary*), 2nd. rev. edn, Edinburgh: T. and T. Clark.

Spender, D. (1980), *Man Made Language*, London: Routledge and Kegan Paul.

Stagg, E. and Stagg, F. (1978), *Woman in the World of Jesus*, Edinburgh: The Saint Andrew Press.

Stanton, E. Cady (ed.) (1895; 1898), *The Woman's Bible* (Part I, 1895; Part II, 1898), Edinburgh: Polygon Books; New York: European Publishing Company (reprinted New York: Arno Press, 1974).

Steinberg, N. (1988), 'Israelite Tricksters, their Analogues and Cross-Cultural Study', in Exum, J. Cheryl and Bos, J.W.H. (eds), 1988, pp.1–13.

Sternberg, M. (1985), *The Poetics of Biblical Narrative: Ideological Literature and the Drama of Reading*, Bloomington: Indiana University Press.

Sternberg, M. (1992), 'Biblical Poetics and Sexual Politics: From Reading to Counterreading', *Journal of Biblical Literature*, **111**, pp.463–88.

Sterring, A. (1994), 'The Will of the Daughters', in Brenner, A. (ed.), 1994c, pp.88–99.

Stone, B.W. (1992), 'Second Isaiah: Prophet to Patriarchy', *Journal for the Study of the Old Testament*, **56**, pp.85–99.

Suleiman, S.R. (1980), 'Introduction: Varieties of Audience-Oriented Criticism', in Suleiman, S.R. and Crosman, I. (eds), pp.3–45.

Suleiman, S.R. and Crosman, I. (eds) (1980), *The Reader in the Text. Essays on Audience and Interpretation*, Princeton: Princeton University Press.

Thistlethwaite, S.B. (1985), 'Every Two Minutes: Battered Women and Feminist Interpretation', in Russell, L.M. (ed.), 1985b, pp.96–107.

Tolbert, M.A. (1983a), 'Defining the Problem: The Bible and Feminist Hermeneutics', in Tolbert, M.A. (ed.), 1983b, pp.113–26.

Tolbert, M.A. (ed.) (1983b), *The Bible and Feminist Hermeneutics* (*Semeia*, **28**), Chico, California: Scholars Press.

Tompkins, J.P. (1980), *Reader-Response Criticism. From Formalism to Post-Structuralism*, Baltimore: The Johns Hopkins University Press.

Trible, Ph. (1973), 'Depatriarchalizing in Biblical Interpretation', *Journal of the American Academy of Religion*, **41**, pp.30–48.

Trible, Ph. (1976), 'Woman in the OT', in Crim, K. (ed.), *The Interpreter's Dictionary of the Bible (Supplementary Volume)*, Nashville: Abingdon, pp.963–6.

Trible, Ph. (1978), *God and the Rhetoric of Sexuality*, London: SCM; Philadelphia: Fortress Press.

Trible, Ph. (1979), 'Eve and Adam: Genesis 2-3 Reread', in Christ, C.P. and Plaskow, J. (eds), pp.74–83.

Trible, Ph. (1984), *Texts of Terror: Literary-Feminist Readings of Biblical Narratives*, Philadelphia: Fortress Press.

Trible, Ph. (1985), 'Postscript: Jottings on the Journey', in Russell, L.M. (ed.), 1985b, pp.147–9.

Trible, Ph. (1989), 'Bringing Miriam out of the Shadows', *Bible Review*, 5, pp.14–25 (reprinted in Brenner, A. (ed.), 1994c, pp.166–86).

Trible, Ph. (1995), 'Eve and Miriam: From the Margins to the Center', in Shanks, H. (ed.), pp.5–24.

Trible, Ph. (2000), 'Miriam', in Meyers, C. (ed.), pp.127–9.

Valler, Shulamit (1999), 'The Story of Jephthah's Daughter in the Midrash', in Brenner, A. (ed.), pp.48–66.

Vaux, R. de (1965), *Ancient Israel: Its Life and Institutions,* 2nd edn, trans. J. McHugh, London: Darton, Longman and Todd; New York: McGraw-Hill.

Vawter, B. (1977), *On Genesis: A New Reading*, London: Geoffrey Chapman.

Vos, C.J. (1968), *Woman in Old Testament Worship*, Delft: Judels and Brinkman.

Wacker, M.-T. (1998), 'Historical, Hermeneutical, and Methodological Foundations', in Schottroff, L., Schroer, S. and Wacker, M.-T. (eds), pp.3–82.

Watson, F. (1994), *Text, Church and World: Biblical Interpretation in Theological Perspective*, Edinburgh: T. and T. Clark.

Weems, R.J. (1995), *Battered Love: Marriage, Sex, and Violence in the Hebrew Prophets*, Minneapolis: Fortress Press.

Westermann, C. (1986), *Genesis 12–36: A Commentary*, trans. J.J. Scullion, London: SPCK; Minneapolis: Augsburg.

Willard, F.E. (1889), *Woman in the Pulpit*, Chicago: Woman's Temperance Publication Association.

Wimsatt, W.K., Jr. (1968), 'Genesis: A Fallacy Revisited', in Demetz, P., Greene, T. and Nelson, L., Jr. (eds), *The Disciplines of Criticism: Essays in Literary Theory, Interpretation and History*, New Haven and London: Yale University Press, pp.193–225.

Wimsatt, W.K., Jr. and Beardsley, M.C. (1946), 'The Intentional Fallacy', *Sewanee Review,* 54, pp.468–88 (reprinted in Wimsatt, W.K., Jr., *The Verbal Icon: Studies in the Meaning of Poetry*, London: Methuen and Company Ltd, 1970, pp.3–18).

Wolde, E. van (1995), 'The Development of Job: Mrs Job as Catalyst', in Brenner, A. (ed.), 1995c, pp.201–21.

Yee, G.A. (1992), 'Hosea', in Newsom, C.A. and Ringe, Sharon H. (eds), pp.195–202.

Yee, G.A. (1995a), '"I Have Perfumed my Bed with Myrrh": The Foreign Woman (*'iššâ zarâ*) in Proverbs 1–9', in Brenner, A. (ed.), 1995c, pp.110–26.

Yee, G.A. (ed.) (1995b), *Judges and Method: New Approaches in Biblical Studies*, Minneapolis: Fortress Press.

Index of Subjects

Index of Modern Authors

Index of Biblical References